Treated Or Tricked?

Alternative Health Therapies Diagnosed

Badu Bediako, B.Sc.; M.Sc.; Ph.D (Biochem)
& Selwyn R. Stevens, Ph.D. (Bib.St.); D.Min.

PUBLISHED BY

Jubilee Resources International Inc.
Equipping Christians, Liberating Captives

Jubilee Resources International Inc.

PO Box 3, Feilding 4740, New Zealand

or our secure Internet Webshop at

www.jubileeresources.org

ISBN 978-0-958341-78-3

Your guarantee of accurate Information: various sources and authorities have been quoted in good faith throughout this book. Every attempt has been made to ensure these quotations are accurate and in context.

The author uses American English spelling, not the Queen's English.

DISCLAIMER:

The authors and Jubilee Resources do not seek to be in conflict with legitimate medical practice. We believe there is ample evidence that human problems, including illness and infirmities are fundamentally spiritual in cause and that associated physiological and psychological manifestations are the symptoms. The information included is intended for general knowledge only, and is not a substitute for medical advice or treatment for specific medical conditions.

CONTENTS

Forewords

"Over the last fifteen years or so, there has been a tremendous upsurge in the availability and usage of Alternative Medical therapies.

Regrettably, for the non-discerning and frequently deceived users, including even ardent Christians, this has all too often not brought the anticipated joyful end-results. Greater household stocks of useless 'medicines' together with smaller bank accounts, may bring testimony to that. Worse still, those folks who place themselves literally in the hands of dubious practitioners, may well find themselves ultimately in a worse condition instead of better. For Christians, this so often means a failure to advance, or even a downturn in their spiritual walk with their Lord and Savior, Jesus Christ. Having been in general medical practise for 34 years, and now some years in Christian counseling ministry, I have seen both sides of the coin, as it were. Unhesitatingly, I would have to say that the manifestation of deception and anger are the greatest prices unsuspecting dabblers in the occult pay.

I congratulate the authors on a well-researched and documented presentation of the facts. This is indeed a very timely book. It should find wide acceptance and frequent reference."

Dr. W. Murray Sare, M.B.; B.S. (Lond.)

Retired General Medical Practitioner, Counsellor,
Te Awamutu, New Zealand.

"I believe this book will be a powerful tool in helping purify the church in readiness to receive our Lord Jesus Christ."

Karen E. Gazley, B.Sc. (Biochemistry & Psychology); M.B.A. N.Z.C.S. (Paramedical); C.O.P. (Biochemistry & Microbiology); Qualified Medical Labroratory Technologist. Wellington, New Zealand

"This book is of divine revelation. It so clearly indicates the root causes of sin, suffering and sickness, and how the Holy Spirit will bring forth release to captives in bondage.

Timely God-given research reveal necessary information and reasons why mankind is so tricked and deceived by the persuasions of the evil one - it's astounding the lengths Satan will go to bring about despair and defeat (but then, he is the thief and the destroyer).

But, praise God, there is no need to live in defeat - because of the Lord Jesus Christ; there is salvation and there is deliverance and victory because of His precious blood shed for us at Calvary. This book will show you the way."

Margaret E. Tredray, N.Z.R.N. & Gold Medalist,
Retired Nursing Tutor, Auckland, New Zealand

Acknowledgements

The authors wish to give special thanks to the medical and scientific panel who reviewed the manuscript of this book, and whose comments, suggestions and encouragement to proceed with this book have been most valued. In addition to the above, the panel included Dr. Richard Turnbull; Dr. Andrew Dominikovich; Dr. Murray Shaw; Dr. Mark McCullough; Dr Christine Rushton; science tutor Brian Caughley; nurses Judy Nicol and Dawn Barrett; and with special gratitude to Gerald Arthur for his excellent proofreading and logic.

Introduction

The reason for this book will become evident by the time the reader has completed it. We have found a high level (a dangerous level in our opinion) of ignorance by Christians - including among many pastors and ministers - of what is broadly known today as "Alternative Health."

Pause for a moment - to ask yourself this question - "Alternative to What?" We believe the answer is alternative to proper scientific and medical health diagnosis, practice and treatment. Normal or orthodox medical treatments and therapies must undergo many rigorous tests to prove they work, and also to determine why they work.

Alternative treatments and therapies do not often work when made to face scientific and medical tests. An example was the series of tests which the top Iridologists in North America were put through. The best these "Professionals" could manage was 2.6% correct diagnosis of patients.[1] Guess work and even rank amateurs might have been better. The real issue from a health perspective is that with such high failure rates, it isn't just a gamble. To put our health and lives in the hands of most Alternative Therapists appears highly dangerous.

However, we are compelled to write this book with an additional reason in mind. It is our contention and concern, backed up by several medical and counseling experts we have consulted in several countries, that some Alternative Health Therapies are major doorways through which people are introduced into occultism and spiritist-related deceptions.

Perhaps we need to spell out the obvious: Our health (and that of our family) is important. The physical and spiritual health of our communities and nations are important. It is important to know if our medical doctor may be using a therapy which involves quackery, or the occult, regardless of whether it works or not. Alternative medicine and therapies are a major vehicle for spreading the occult, as will be shown. As such, its world-view is definitely anti-Christian. In addition, Alternative Therapists frequently promote an irrational attitude to other areas of life, not just medicine.

This book is written by Christians primarily for Christians, although we believe it will be relevant and helpful to those with other beliefs. We are aware of some religious leaders who recommend and even teach or use some of the therapies we will discuss here. We humbly request such folk to pray through the issues we present, and invite them to turn away from everything which is shown to be contrary to God's Word, the Bible, and which are also frequently contrary to both science and commonsense. We know of several who have already done so as the result of our earlier publications and seminars.

A number of Christian medical doctors and counselors have told of the almost violent physical response from Christian patients when their doctor has recommended they stop treatment from Alternative Therapists because of the physical, emotional and sometimes spiritual dangers. This suggests that people deeply rooted in some practices in Alternative Medicine may already be victims of emotional, physical or spiritual disorders.

Let us now define our terminology so there is no confusion as to what we mean.

We will use the term "Alternative Therapist" or "Alternative Therapy" to mean all those practitioners or practices which go under titles such as "New Age," "Holistic," "Complementary," and/or "Alternative." This covers a large variety of practices and beliefs, and the primary thing they have in common is that they are not taught in a Western orthodox medical school. Alternative Therapies are not taught in those schools because they do not pass the test of scientific proof. Anecdotal or subjective opinion are insufficient.

We will use the term "Medical Doctor" to mean all practitioners who have been trained in those Western orthodox medical schools which utilise only those therapies or practices which have undergone scientific tests, which are not only proven to work, but do so for evident valid reasons. "Disease" is detrimental physical change which occurs in the body which may or may not be detectable by a doctor, and is not a result of simple aging. (Age produces much change which is not called disease.) "Illness" is how we as individuals manifest disease. "Medicine" is the art of restoring and preserving health, especially by means of remedial substances etc. as distinct from surgery.

The World Health Organization stated in 1946 that health is *"Not just the absence of disease but the state of complete physical, mental and social wellbeing."* A more practical definition from a New Zealand medical school is "the optimum adaptation of the individual to his environments; physical, psychological and social."

Please consider this statement - If something is true, it can stand being questioned. But if it is not true, then it needs to be questioned. If a certain type of Alternative Therapy is good and true, then let us confirm that. If any deceive or harm people, then we must reveal that. It is readily admitted that Christians have not always explained the issues on this subject very well, and that sometimes their zeal to warn of consequences hasn't always been balanced with compassion. We do not seek to attack or belittle any individual practitioner of Alternative Health practices in this book or anywhere else. We seek to reveal the truth about beliefs and practices, and to explain the consequences - both positive and negative - so that an informed choice can be made. Many people need to make better healthcare choices than they have been. We want to help those who probably don't know that they are doing the wrong or potentially dangerous thing, especially in the area of Alternative Therapies. God really loves the people who are under deception, but He does not love the deception. He wants us to know the truth, so that the truth will set us free (John 8:32).

World-Views

Our theological or philosophical world-view is the foundation we have for virtually everything else we believe as human beings. It makes a huge difference to our conduct and lives whether or not we believe we are answerable to a creator God.

The Bible View

The Bible records that God took the initiative in creating the world and all the good things it contains, including human life. Mankind was created by God for one primary reason - to have fellowship, a relationship or friendship with God. God doesn't need us, but we need Him. God sets the rules which govern His creation. Some are natural rules or laws (such as gravity) while others are spiritual and moral rules or laws, and all have a purpose. For example, if we ignore the law of gravity when walking along the top of a cliff, we could hurt or even kill ourselves. The same applies if we ignore or reject God's spiritual and moral laws. For example, sexual promiscuity brings a considerable cost, not least in diseases - physical or emotional. Worshipping anything other than the One True God is idolatry, for which God warns He will judge those involved. (It has been observed that people take on the likeness of the gods they worship or serve.)

Following Adam and Eve's sin which caused the breaking of the human relationship with God, it has been God Himself who has tried to restore the relationship. Firstly He showed us that we human beings are incapable of keeping the Law, including the Ten Commandments. He also showed us that the animal sacrifices for the atoning of our sins didn't work for long because we humans kept on sinning. Finally He sent His only Son, Jesus Christ. He didn't come just to teach great moral lessons for us to follow, although He did do that. His primary purpose was to Atone for your sins and ours, to pay the penalty which all our sins deserve, and thereby allow the relationship between God and mankind to be restored. God sets the conditions, which is His right as creator. If He states that we must avoid certain things such as occultism, divination, etc., because they are a danger and a snare to us, then He does so with our best interests at heart. After all, He loves each one of us enough to send Jesus to pay for our sins. We ought to be grateful and eager receive His offer of eternal life.

The Bible world perspective or view is that we are a spirit, we have a soul (our mind, emotions, and will, etc.) and we also have a body during our single lifetime. (See Genesis 1; & 1 Thessalonians 5:23.) For those in covenant relationship with Jesus Christ, our spirits and souls are eternal, and following our life, death and resurrection, go on to the reward of living with Jesus for eternity, when we each receive a new imperishable body, (see 1 Corinthians 15). Those who didn't comply with God's requirements for eternal life will spend eternity without Him, and face punishment in an unpleasant place never intended for human beings.

Occult/Spiritist View

This view include all spiritual activities and beliefs which reject or disobey God's instructions in the Bible. When the God of the Bible states frequently that He alone is the one True God, and that all others are only pretenders to truth and power, the onus is on each of us to either accept or reject that, and to face any consequences which arise from our choice. The general occult world view is that we are mind, spirit and then body, with the emphasis in that order. There is a strong emphasis on the superiority of the mind over the body and the spirit.

Humanist View

Humanism believes there are no spiritual answers to the questions of life - no Creator God, no divine influence to guide, judge or bless, no spiritual perspective to consider whatever. There is no deity, whether good or evil, and we must make our own way in life. Life for a Humanist - taken to its logical conclusion - is actually meaningless and selfish, because everything is centred on self, the big ME! The "I come first" syndrome. Ultimately such a life must end in despair or disappointment, for there is nothing to hope for. Humanism has no answer about "WHY" life exists. However it encompasses a wide range of philosophies and therapies which state that your future and your health depend on you alone.

Healing Categories

There are six basic categories of body healing.

1. NATURAL - the body heals itself because of built-in immune and repair systems installed by the manufacturer (God). There are ailments and sicknesses for which you don't need to take any medicine because God has programed the body in such a way that for many viral or bacterial infections the body can take care of those. In fact, many of us have had diseases we weren't even aware of. Unless an illness is serious, most people usually recover whether they visit a doctor or not. The human body has been designed with a marvellous array of immune systems and automatic healing processes. For example, when you cut your hand while peeling an apple, it doesn't stay cut. The blood clots and seals the leak, otherwise you would bleed to death. (A few people do have an impairment of blood clotting due to a deficiency in their make-up, but these are comparatively rare.) After the blood clots, a scab forms, allowing new skin tissue to grow, and the old dead tissue finally falls off. If the finger were cut on a print, the new tissue has the same pattern as the old. This is an example of God's attention to the many wonders of our bodies. Some healing restores the damaged area to its original condition; some healing leaves scarring because the body may not always heal itself completely.

2. MEDICAL - Medical Healing is where a doctor intervenes and conditions your body in such a way that your body heals itself. If it is an infection, an antibiotic is administered to help the body to defeat the infection. In many conditions, medicine doesn't actually heal; it controls the disease process, e.g., diabetes, asthma, high blood pressure, etc. Sometimes drugs, some of which originated as herbal remedies, are used. If there is a need for surgery, the surgeon comes in and cuts off some of the damaged tissue. Although some treatments have side effects, the efficacy of generally accepted modern-day surgical and medical treatment is such that when a treatment is given, it is given because the individual is highly likely to fare worse were a treatment not be given. In a nutshell, medical healing saves far more lives than it loses.

Medical healing cannot heal everything. Huge advances are being made as our God-given minds search for new medicines and understanding of illness. But people still suffer, despite the best of medical care. It is no wonder, then, that many are tempted to seek help from other therapies, especially for chronic conditions. In this fallen world we hope and seek for wholeness of our disease-prone bodies, and it is hard to accept that some symptoms cannot be helped by medical science. But we must not be caught up in lies and deception - promises of healing which may be false, or worse, will cost us our souls.

3. DIVINE - Divine Healing is where the sick person calls on God and He heals them. Many Christians have experienced that kind of healing, where you call for the elders of the church and they come and lay hands on you, anoint you with oil and they pray for you and the sickness goes away. (See James 5:14-16, Mark 16:15-18, Psalm 103:1-5.)

The Bible is full of instances where God healed people. He also provides a "Gift of Healing" (1 Corinthians 12:9) so Divine Healing continues today. Such healings are often miraculous. Dealing effectively with causes, such as stress, unforgiveness, broken relationships (including with God) etc. can bring healing. This method should not be confused with so-called "Faith Healing," which involves human mind over matter principles, hypnotic suggestion and/or psychic powers.

4. QUACKERY- A quack healer is someone who falsely pronounces you as healed when you haven't been, or, they fraudulently misrepresent their ability and experience to diagnose and treat disease, or to explain the effects of the treatment offered. This happens in some spiritual groups, including some Christian churches (most evident in what are often called the "hyperfaith" churches that misunderstand the difference between faith and presumption).

Quackery may best to explained as a misrepresentation of diagnostic or treatment ability; falsely claiming experience in that; ignorance or dishonesty concerning medical skill; the practice of medicine by unlicensed individuals; and/or the use of methods not generally recognised by the medical profession, (usually because the evidence of why a therapy or practice works is lacking).

Orthodox medical people and Alternative Therapists alike know that for most sicknesses, if you allow some time to elapse, the body frequently takes care of itself. Quack healers capitalize on that. (More about these later.)

"... Holistic medicine is not a scientific tradition. It has no paradigmatic work, no recognized set of problems, and no shared standards for what constitutes a solution to those problems; it also lacks the critical exchange among its practitioners that is characteristic of the sciences," wrote Drs. Stalker and Glymour in their book, ***"Examining Holistic Medicine."*** They went on to comment, *"The shared aims that tie so many diverse people together are to institutionalise holistic medical practices, and, furthermore, to loosen the demands of evidence that we, as a society, impose on those who claim to cure or prevent disease. The first aim requires the second... Only by abandoning the usual criteria of scientific evidence, and even the usual demands of rational thinking, can the claim of holistic medicants be established and made whole... The science of holistic medicine is bogus;... the philosophical views championed by this movement are incoherent, uninformed and unintelligent; ... Most holistic therapies are crank in the usual sense of that word: they lack any sound scientific basis."*

When competent academics who are medically and scientifically trained and experienced investigate the journals of the Alternative/Holistic communities, they find a serious shortage of proven tests. Let us mention just one example. Dr. Thomas Chalmers is Distinguished Service Professor of Medicine, and Dean Emeritus of Mount Sinai School of Medicine. He has authored over 250 publications and is head of the Clinical Trials unit of Mt. Sinai Medical Centre. Dr. Chalmers examined the scientific claims of articles in the most scientifically oriented new age medical journal, ***"The Journal of Holistic Medicine"*** - the official journal of the American Holistic Medical Association. After examining forty-seven articles from four different volumes, Dr. Chalmers discovered only nine trials of therapies, and of these only two were randomized controlled trials, both by the same author. Dr. Chalmers reported that the scientific tests were few and far between and "generally not well done." They suffered from errors such as *"a lack of adequate control with regard to measurements and separation of investigative agents."* Dr. Chalmers went on the comment that this Journal has a long way to go to achieve the same standards of scientific reporting as the more orthodox medical journals require. Since "The Journal of Holistic Medicine" is the top scientific publication in the field of Alternative medicine, we believe the point is well proven.

Holistic health means body, soul and spirit, so if someone claims to be a holistic health practitioner, they are claiming to be able to heal people's spirits and souls. This is not directly associated with medical science. If the result is a spiritual healing, then the obvious question which must be asked is "Which medical school, Bible college or seminary did you learn this method of spiritual healing from?" The Bible speaks in James 5:14-16 about healing and 1 Corinthians 12 about the Gift of Healing which is imparted by God. Completing a diploma from a quack school over a couple of weekend workshops which cost a few hundred or a thousand dollars can never be equal to a recognised medical degree.

Regarding this area of quackery, the work of Dr. Kurt Koch, one of the most prominent Christian psychologists, researchers and authors, is worthy of note. He wrote, *"No genuine healing occurs, but rather merely a transference of the condition from the physical to the emotional, or spiritual realm. There are numerous cases of suicides, fatal accidents, emotional disorders, diseases strokes and insecurity are to observed among such practices."*[2] (Dr. Koch has investigated over 20,000 cases.)

We should never do anything intended to enhance one part of our being which will cripple or destroy another part. A healing for your physical body which has the potential of killing the soul or the spirit just isn't worth it!

5. OCCULT - Many, perhaps most of the New Age/Alternative Health Therapies involve Eastern religions, Buddhism, Hinduism and Taoism. These are now practised openly in Western culture. One of the obvious areas of these practices is open Satanic worship, which is evident throughout the world and in many cultures. In the New Age, Spiritist practices involve the old type of occultism and divination, which God strongly condemns in the Bible. Different aspects of divination involve include soothsaying, Tarot cards and ouija boards and dream interpretations. But there is something new these days: there is a drift towards the study of ancient religions and the practices that these ancient people used in Satan worship, although this can be disguised to the unwary.

One of the major areas where New Age occultism is very prominent these days is in health. Some people hold the belief that Satan does not do anything good. They claim that all truth and all knowledge belong to God, so as long as it works is must be good and it must come from God. There are a lot of things that work in this world, but they are not of God. Abortion works, it gets rid of the fetus: but it is not of God because He values life. We need to weigh everything carefully with the Word of God and see what is of God and what is not of Him.

Occult Healing is where demons heal people. Sometimes this is called an "Energy" or "Life Force." Evil spirits do heal. That may sound strange to some people. One of the many areas in which demons operate is in healing and also in the area of telling the future. One of the authors comes from that kind of culture in Africa, where he has seen a lot of demonic healing. You may ask, "How can a demon do something good?" Well, eventually you will pay for it, for there is a price to be paid when you subject yourself to demonic healing. Spiritualism is involved. Jesus Christ warns us about such deceptions, (see Matthew 24:24; & Revelation 13:13).

Categories 4 and 5 above constitute the vast majority of New Age or alternative healing methods. Many researchers, authors and counsellors from many parts of the world are now saying that Alternative Therapies are a major vehicle for the spread of occultism today. [3]

Here are some of the key founders and/or leading users of Alternative healing Therapies who are or have been involved in some form of spiritism or occult activity during their lifetimes.

Founder/Guru	**Occult Activity**
Rudolf Steiner	Anthroposophic Medicine
Elmer & Alyce Green	Biofeedback
D. D. & B. J. Palmer	Chiropractic
Bernard Jensen	Iridology
George Goodheart	Applied Kinesiology
Wilhelm Reich	Orgonomy
Samuel Hahnemann	Homeopathy
Randolf Stone	Polarity Therapy
Robert Assagoili	Psychosynthesis
Dolores Kreiger & Dora Kunz	Therapeutic Touch
Mike Samuel	Modern Visualization
Albert Abrams & George De la Warr	Radionics

Also Edgar Cayce, Emanuel Swedenborg, and many others.

6. EMOTIONAL - This is a healing which attempts to deal with symptoms rather than the causes. One might call it "Mind-over-Matter" healing, because there can be physical improvements for a while. This gradually wears off and the condition returns. The end result is that the person is no better off than before. This does happen in quite a number of healing services in churches as a soulish attempt to duplicate Divine Healing. Some people want to be healed regardless of the costs, even if they haven't met the conditions which God insists on first.

There are a lot of people who consult practices classified as "Christian homeopaths," "Christian yoga," "Christian self-esteem teachers," for treatment. The "Christian" label lures many needy people into their care. We need to know the forces/powers behind these practices so we can know ourselves, and then inform other people who are trapped in some of these practices. Great care should be taken with those who label themselves or their practice "Christian". Check to see if this is real, or just a convenient front. Good spiritual fruit should be obvious, and opposition to occult practices will be the first things to check.

A Background to the problem

What is this Alternative Health or New Age medicine? Basically it is the philosophies and practices of the New Age occultism applied in the area of health. Sometimes it is called New Age medicine, sometimes you may come across the word "holistic" health movement, holistic in the sense that they claim to heal the body, the soul and the spirit. Deuteronomy 20:16-18 warns us not to serve a lie. The Lord requires us as Believers, because we have Christ in our lives, to stay away from the practices of unbelievers. We cannot take that which is evil and "polish it up" so we can give it to God. He won't accept it. For true Christians, there must be a total separation from the practices of the New Age and many aspects of the Alternative Health area.

We believe the New Age Alternative Therapies come with an all-embracing promise of spiritual fulfillment and harmony. These practices have even entered into some Christian churches. Often people do not want to talk about it, because they might offend someone, or sound too negative, or judgmental.

Alternative/New Age Health Therapies do cause people to become interested in New Age in general. It is a sort of recruiting ground where people are encouraged to get involved in the thoughts, philosophies and occult practices of New Age. One of the authors, a counsellor, had a woman come for counseling with serious problems, including deep depression. She said she was taking special lessons on herbal treatments. I told her she would have many problems there. She said *"It was just knowledge of herbs."* Well, I know that God created herbs to be used, but often the way New Age people use it these days you have to be very careful. Using a Word of Knowledge (1 Corinthians 12:8) I asked, *"That hall where you take your lessons, are there any pictures or publications of lesbianism?"* She answered, "*Oh yes, that is the last thing they are going to teach us.*" These New Age training programmes are frequently recruiting grounds. The first phase is to expose people to a New Age practice. After that, if you are a woman, they will attempt to get you involved in some aspect of lesbianism and feminism, and then the next step is into occultism, it really is a very short step. These are cleverly designed steps to convert a person to a lifestyle they might previously have rejected. It is subtle - but sneaky!

But they won't tell you this. They will only tell you they are training you to use herbs.

We believe herbs can be used to cure certain illnesses. If you know that a particular herb can heal someone, you can use it if proper precautions are taken. But what is happening now in the Alternative Therapy scene is very dangerous, and we would advise people involved in herbal treatments to be very cautious of who gives you the herb or where you get them from. There is a deliberate attempt to hide the religious aspect of New Age health and Alternative Therapies and medicine, and it is done in many ways. They sometimes add "Christian" to it, or they may use lengthy scientific terminology. Instead of telling you that the "force is going to heal you," such as Yin and Yang from ancient Chinese Taoism, they tell you that "We are just dealing with your sympathetic and parasympathetic nervous system." It sounds so scientific that to the ordinary person it must appear good. But there is nothing scientific about what they are doing. There is a cover-up, a camouflage, sometimes through ignorance, but more often through deceit.

New Age medicine is opposed to modern science because science has repeatedly proved most Alternative Therapies to be false, and often not to be effective. The interesting thing is that when it is subjected to scientific investigation it is proved that it doesn't work, but when patients go to Alternative Therapists it works. The question is "What makes it work?" There is definitely a spiritual dimension involved in most of these practices, and that is what makes them work. There is occultic healing taking place. So you find that spiritism is found in Alternative Therapies such as Acupuncture, Dreamwork, Meditation, psychic diagnosis and healing, hypnotic and Past-life regression, color healing, radionics, pendulum dowsing, visualization, homeopathy, crystal healing, and much much more.

New Age philosophy is deeply rooted in ancient Chinese, Indian, American Indian and Third World (especially African) voodoo and occultism. You can go to the shopping areas in any major city in the world. Look for the sign of the rainbow on some "health" shops. If you count the rainbow colours - it isn't seven (like nature's one) it is usually five or six. This is often a sign of New Age shops. A casual glance around will show you a shop for Iridology, where they read your eyeballs. Formerly they used to read palms, now they read eyeballs. You will probably also find a massage shop, a feminist shop, and many others. These days we have noticed the sign of the rainbow has often been removed, so people must be getting to know where they are. They also deal in all kinds of diet food.

Science & Alternative Disease Theories

Medical Science has now categorized the different ways the body can have things go wrong. Briefly these are:

Trauma: Throughout history we humans have been subjected to various health problems caused by war, natural disasters, animal attacks and falls. Exhumations of mummies and similar aged human remains show missing limbs, healed fractures and embedded weapons. In more recent history, we have a tendency to experience sports injuries, motor vehicle and aeroplane accidents. The down side of the discovery of fire gave us burns, while we have an inventiveness for tools which leave us with wounds from their use and misuse. As Dr. Hendrik Visser pointed out in his book ***"Healing For Your Hurts,"*** *"The very technologies that helped extend our lives also threatened to shorten them."* [38]

Genetics: Many conditions from high blood pressure and heart disease to Down's Syndrome, Cystic Fibrosis and Huntington's Disease fall into this category. For some there is an extra chromosome, for others there is Mendal's theory of heredity by genes, and for yet others there can be defects in genes such as congenital heart disease or cleft palate.

Degeneration: As we grow older, things begin to wear out. Skin loses elasticity, and begins to wrinkle. Our eye lenses thicken resulting in far-sightedness and decreased vision, called macular degeneration. Our hearing is affected, losing the ability to hear the higher-pitched tones. Taste and smell receptors decrease in effectiveness, and muscles lose mass while bones become riddled with cavities, causing some to break with the slightest fall or knock. Lung capacity reduces and the heart, kidneys and other organs become less able to handle their appointed tasks.

Infections: We are increasingly attacked by viruses, bacteria, fungal infections and parasite infestations. Epidemics are becoming increasingly common, and our resistance to them is declining.

Covid-19, SARS, Asian Bird Flu, HIV/Aids, Ebola and the various Hepatitis strains have the potential to dwarf the Influenza epidemic which killed millions around the world in 1918. Research is ongoing to try and prevent these and other epidemics from gaining a foothold in the human and animal populations.

Altered Immunity: Science is beginning to unravel why the body starts developing antibodies against it's own tissues. Immune systems can be misdirected to react, causing allergies. Everything from pollen, dust mites, bee or wasp stings, peanuts, milk, soy or wheat products and even exposure to certain clothing fabrics can cause an allergic reaction, resulting in itchy eyes, runny noses, asthma or hives, and can in some cases cause anaphylactic shock resulting in death.

Neoplasia: This is the name for cells which multiply uncontrollably, causing cancers and tumours. Often this is caused by genetic mutation at chromosome level. There are many potential causes for these being researched now, including the role of carcinogens, viruses, radiation, chemical toxins and tobacco smoke.

Psychological: It has been estimated that about half of the visits to a doctor are for illnesses caused by our minds. Depression, insomnia, family problems, stress and much more are frequently the symptoms of a wide range of conditions which affect our health. We are beginning to understand the connection between emotional pain due to sexual or ritual abuse, unexpected bereavement, rejection and abandonment, marital strife and much more.

Nutritional: The quality of most Western diets is declining, due in large part to the commercialisation of food production, and the resulting loss of essential nutrients. Vitamins and other Supplements have become a huge industry, in part due to this fundamental change, and the organic market is growing as a partial response. Many people suffer from nutritional disorders. Obesity is close to epidemic levels in North America and elsewhere, and the high salt/sodium intake is causing hardened arteries resulting in high blood pressure, and excessive fat intake is causing much of the heart attacks and strokes.

Environmental: From the air we breath (especially in large car-filled cities) to the water supply with its increasing need for chemical additions to make it "safe"; from noise in the workplace to the decaying ozone layer, and the electromagnetic radiation from high voltage power lines, we are under increasing attack.

Alternative Disease Theory: There are three primary causes of disease, according to Alternative Therapists. These are all based on loss of balance, or homoeostasis. Dr. Hendrik Visser states accurately, *"They believe that health is maintained by a balance within the body and mind of either internal or external energies, substances or structures. Generally they theorise a loss of homoeostasis in either the spiritual, biochemical or structural areas. Therapies are then directed toward re-establishing homoeostasis in the area of presumed imbalance."* [38]

The spiritual area involves Traditional Chinese Medicine, Ayurveda (Hindu), Therapeutic Touch, Reiki, and more (see section on Energy, page 31).

The biochemical area covers perceived deficient or excessive nutrients, intolerances to various foods or the environment, or excessive toxins which they believe are affecting the body's ability to resist disease.

The structural area includes such practices as traditional Chiropractic, Osteopathy and some massage therapies which began with foundational beliefs in energy healing with a strong psychic component. As mentioned elsewhere, not all these therapies are suspect in their use by those therapists who have rejected the occult roots to them.

Factors That Favor Alternative Therapists

1. Time: Alternative Therapists often take more time than most medical doctors.

2. Compassion: Alternative Therapists are often seen as more caring because they take more time, and often seem more interested in the whole person, including the soul and spirit element and not just the disease.

3. Touch: Most Alternative Therapists use touch. Touch is an important way to communicate concern and compassion, which medical practitioners often appear to neglect.

4. The inability of medical science to heal everything: The vast majority of Alternative Therapies used on people are for non life-threatening conditions. It has been stated that the main reasons for people seeking help from Alternative Therapists are related to the relief of symptoms, mostly pain, from musculoskeletal disorders, and relief from emotional distress without recourse to tranquillizers. What people are looking for is a safe, easy to use approach that can be undertaken at home together with self-help programmes to improve wellbeing. It is recognized that not all medical treatment produces the results of improved health we may desire. Orthodox medicine doesn't always satisfy. It must be recognised that much of modern medicine is crisis-focused, with the main weapons being the pill and the scalpel.

5. The "Magic" of Alternative Medicine: Ordinary medicine has become familiar to most people and it is important for some people for their practitioner to appear "Magical.' One Alternative Therapist described it, "The strange words and unfamiliar practices convey an atmosphere of a magical cult, which was a very powerful healing force," [4]

Many Alternative Health Therapists seem to have a more personal and less clinical "bedside manner." In contrast many scientific health professionals have the appearance of "business" and even starchiness or distance from the patients. This can be off-putting, since when we are unwell we are most in need of a friendly approach, a sense of being understood - and especially the hope that things will be all right. Alternative Therapists give the appearance of understanding these issues better than many scientifically-trained health professionals. Alternative Therapists often involve the patient to a much greater degree than medical doctors. After all, patients should be active participants in their own health care, rather than passive bystanders watching the medicos poke and prod, then give a pill prior to moving on to the next person.

These five factors speak of people's perceptions, and may differ from what is true. It is recognized that over the past decades there has been considerable improvements in medical training. Amongst the positive trends there is a greater awareness of stress-related illnesses which can be attributed to our emotional and mental state. One doctor told us that while he was at medical school, he was taught to "comfort always, relieve often and cure sometimes." In many countries around the world there have been significant advances in patient's charters and patient's rights, These can be a bit scary to doctors. Many of these charters also apply to Alternative Therapists as well.

Most Alternative Therapists do start off with a desire to help people. Over a period of time what they do often becomes commercialized, and a deception appears to take them over, resulting in what some describe as "Mammon-control" or "Karma for Cash." It must be admitted this is true of some orthodox medical doctors as well.

Before we move on, it is important to look at types of research and their value, particularly with regard to Alternative Therapies. The following table should help understand the issues.

Type of Research	**Hierarchy of Evidence**
Large randomized clinical trials	Highest
Small randomized clinical trials	
Uncontrolled trials	
Observational studies	
Case reports	
Anecdotes	Lowest

Anecdotes include historical usage of a remedy or practise. It may record what happens, but not why. Some continue to use remedies which have been around for decades, even centuries, but that may be due to there being nothing else available. Some have a cultural basis - Acupuncture would be an example for those of Chinese extraction. (It has recently been reported to me from a retired Christian missionary to the Chinese, that when they became Christians, one of the earlier things they repented of and renounced was Acupuncture, due to it's occultic roots.)

I remember being told that if you get burned, whether by cooking or a spark from the fire, or even while doing the ironing, to put butter on the burn immediately. Now we know that the grease from the butter may actually make the recovery from a burn longer and more painful, than putting cold water - not ice - on the burn.

Energy - The Psychic Unifier

The vast majority of Alternative Health Therapists and also those in Human Potential Movements have a unifying factor: the idea of **"Energy."** But what is this energy? There are several types of energy available, not all of them safe. For example, there are electromagnetic, gravitational and nuclear energies. These are scientifically detectable and can be measured. Some minerals, such as plutonium, uranium, radium, and others used in nuclear fission, are clearly toxic to the human body. However, what about quartz crystals which New Agers and other occultists hang around their necks or put in their windows claiming to bring "healing power" to bear on their bodies? Does such an energy exist? We believe this energy has only ever been assumed, but never proven by any recognized scientific methodology. "Energy" as applied by Alternative Health Therapists cannot be identified as "natural" or "neutral," but it can be used for good or evil. Because it causes psychic powers to be developed in the practitioners, and can be transferred from person to person, and because it only seems to fit into a monistic and pantheistic world-view, [5] it can be clearly demonstrated as unscientific and anti-Christian. We believe it can be shown to be firmly rooted in Spiritism and other forms of occultism.

Any serious study of the Bible shows that supernatural energy can only come from only one of two sources - God, or Satan. God often gives people His power and it is seen in the miracles recorded in the Bible and is still seen today in Bible-based Healing ministries. (Both authors practice this.) The energy here comes from God. It isn't latent in the person God is working through. There is no reputable scientific proof that humans have latent, natural, neutral energies available to be developed. Apart from God any supernatural "energy" must come from Satan. There are over 90 different names used to describe psychic energies, and almost without exception they involve spiritist or animistic beliefs. For the past 300 years virtually all "inventors/ users" of this psychic energy were deeply involved in the occult as mediums, psychic researchers or parapsychologists. Here are a few of the better known

ENERGY NAME	USER/INVENTOR	INVOLVEMENT
Astral Light	H.P. Blavatsky	medium/Theosophist
Etheric Formative Forces occultist		Rudolf Steiner
Munia/Mumia	Paracelsus	occultist
Animal Magnetism	F.A. Mesmer	occultist
Spiritus	Robert Fludd	Rosicrucian
Psychic Force	William Crooks	psychic researcher
Biomagnetism	George De La Warr	medium
Ectoplasm	Charles Reicher	psychic researcher
Bioplasma etc.	Viktor Inyushin (& others)	parapsychologist

The overwhelming evidence is that psychic energy requires a spirit or demon to operate it. Human users may falsely believe they have special powers within themselves. Shamans, witchdoctors, Hindu holy men (like Satha Sai Baba) and many others willingly admit they have no powers themselves, but acknowledge their power or energy comes exclusively from the spirits. God forbids human involvement in the occult/spirit realm. Any such contact is with forces and beings alien and hostile to Him. Those involved come into contact with demonic spirits. If you are or have been involved in any practices which include psychic energy you have now been warned about their true nature and the consequences. We aren't being judgemental here, but attempting to warn people of the consequences of involvements which God says will invoke His judgement. Any reader who has been involved in these occultic practices is urged to confess it as a sin before God, repent (which means turn away and stop doing it) and then receive God's forgiveness.

There are two false views held by people about the spiritual realities of evil. First is the view that there is none, it is only imagined or a superstitious myth, and we should ignore it. The second false view is that of obsession - an unhealthy interest or preoccupation with evil or the paranormal. The truth is that such a spiritual realm does exist, and we need to be informed and equipped to deal with it and to keep it in its proper place - submitted to the name and authority of Jesus Christ.

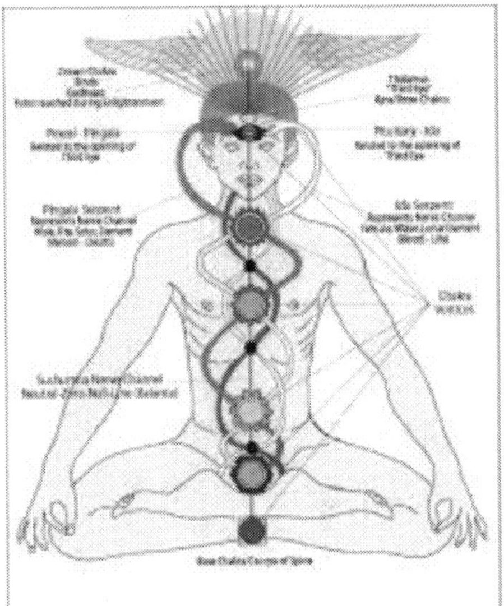

The 7 Chakras of Prana Energy

Prana and Ch'i

The two best known psychic energies are Prana and Ch'i. Both are claimed to be the "essential vital force" of all creation. In other words the universe is god, and since we humans are part of the universe it follows we must be part of god. These concepts cannot be separated from their occultic roots.

Prana is the Hindu/Yogic energy involving the potentially lethal rising of the serpent Kundalini. It is claimed to reside at the base of the spine and is aroused through Yoga. As it rises towards the Middle Eye on the forehead it opens Chakras and gives psychic powers. These are claimed to enable the user to control their mind and body and even the whole universe, thus they become god or part of god. According to Vivekananda "mind healers, faith healers, Spiritualists, Christian Scientists, hypnotists and so on... (have) at the back of each, the control of Prana, whether they know it or not." Wilson and Weldon say "Prana is truly a demonic energy output in seances, witchcraft, psychokinesis, psi-healing etc." [6] The experience of the authors is that Chakras are the nests where the evil spirits dwell.

The Taoists of ancient China believed in the existence of an energy they called "Ch'i." (The Japanese call it Ki.) They claimed it flowed through all the universe (including human bodies and organs) along invisible energy lines called meridians. The Yin and the Yang are the two opposing yet harmonizing forces which are claimed to control this energy. They do not cancel each other out nor are they antagonistic. They are parts of the whole

Yin & Yang Symbol

Yin		Yang	
dark	yielding	light	firm
moon	west/north	sun	east/south
night	metal	day	wood
cold	white/black	heat	green/red
water	rest	fire	movement
dampness	spring/summer	dryness	autumn/winter
feminine (wife)	interior	masculine (husband)	exterior
below	contraction	above	expansion

These believers claim that if an imbalance between Yin and Yang should occur, then illness results. Acupuncture, reflexology and a number of other related "zone therapies" were developed to treat this imbalance and to help restore harmony and healing. This is psychic healing, or in other words they use supernatural energy empowered by an evil spirit.

Ch'i imbalances or disturbances are believed by Taoist practitioners to be caused by an unbalanced diet, emotional disturbances, and climatic conditions during hot or cold weather. They will often prescribe a diet and suggest exercise programme postures to sit or stand, and even the way you should sleep, to influence the flow of Ch'i.

According to the Taoists and New Age occultists, they can manipulate your body to release the "blockage of energy" in your system and then you can become well. Most Alternative Therapists do body manipulation, massages and even diagnostic procedures, so that by the time you come out of the clinic you feel different. Something has happened to you. What they call "Energy" has been put into you.

But the energy they are describing is not a natural or scientific energy. The energy they put into you is a demon. They channel a spirit into your body. We believe that is why they want to put their hands on you. It makes you feel different, because when a spirit is channeled into a human body, it causes a number of changes, including psychological and physiological, and these can even change your blood pressure so you feel different. You can feel excited, and think "I'm okay, surely this practitioner has done something to me." He hasn't done anything more than demonize you, put an evil spirit into you. You see this kind of practice happen in Acupuncture, Acupressure, Applied Kinesiology (muscle-testing), and Therapeutic Touch, to name just a few.

The energy, we want to emphasize again, is not a normal physical energy, and neither is it Holy Spirit energy. You may go to a "Christian" Alternative Therapist, and he may tell you "This is Holy Spirit energy," but it almost certainly is not. The "energies" sound very scientific, but the various practitioners are just talking about demons of the same name known in many cultures by various names.

Culture/Practice	**Name of Energy**
Hinduism	"Prana"
Taoism	"Ch'i'"
American Indians	"Arenda"
Polynesians	"Mana"
Chiropractors	"Innate"
Homeopaths	"Vital Energy"
Yoga	"Kundalini Energy"
Parapsychologists	"Bioplasma"
	"Orgone Energy"
	"Inner Teacher"
	"Powers from the Higher Mind"
	"Latent Human Potential"
	"Archetypes" among others.

The Bible has something to say about this. **"Now the Spirit says expressly that in the latter times people shall depart from the faith, giving heed to seducing spirits, and doctrines of demons,"** (1 Timothy 4:1).

Alternative Therapists are often psychics and occultists. For example, if a psychic Chiropractor manipulates your spine, often what he will do is channel a demon into your body through your spine, and it causes a lot of occult transformations in your body. The therapy may cause you to develop psychic power, and can lead to spirit possession or oppression.

We need to say here that not all practitioners of New Age medicine are psychic. Not all of them are occult either. There are a small proportion of Homeopaths and other Alternative Therapists that do not directly operate in the occult realm. But what happens is that the practice can expose you to a demon that can enter you. Someone came to one of the authors for counseling. This person was having serious problems, including headaches, migraines and depressive conditions. We went through a whole lot of things and I couldn't really pick out what the problem was. So I asked, *"Have you been to any Alternative Health Therapist?"* She said, *"Yes, I've been to an Acupuncturist."* I asked if she saw him pray over the needles before using them, and she said *"Yes."* That was where the problem originated. There was a transfer of spirits into her body. We were able to deal with that by casting out the demon from her body and she remains free to this day. **"For of this sort are those who creep into households and make captives of gullible women loaded down with sins, led away by various lusts, always learning and never able to come to the knowledge of the truth,"** (2 Timothy 3:6-7).

There is a therapy called Chakra healing. The practitioner channels a demon from his chakra (chakras are supposed to be the centers of energy, but are actually the centres where the demons operate from) so he channels a demon into his patient and sometimes it manifests as an energy in the patient's body. This energy transmission creates a lot of physiological response. This can be scientifically monitored. The blood vessels dilate, and result in a flush and you can actually see physical changes in the person's face.

Exposure to Alternative Therapies could result in you getting into the occult, spiritism and witchcraft and then you will come under the condemnation of God. You aren't the only one who is going to pay the price, your children will pay the price, your grand children will pay for it, and even your great-grand children (see Exodus 20:5). These become ancestral curses. (See page 107.)

In Deuteronomy 18:9-13, God lists those practices He clearly forbids. These include divination, sorcery and witchcraft; and in Galatians 5:21 God repeats that people involved in such things will not be part of the Kingdom of God. We are astounded at the impudence of some Christians who contend that God has given us Iridology, Colour Therapy, and other practices which involve divination so that we may be healed. Why would God forbid something, and then turn around and provide the very thing He forbade? He judges the rebellious, and we believe Christians involved in these practices should repent while they have the opportunity.

Wherever you come across terms such as *Cosmic Energy* you will understand the concept better if you replace them with words like psychic or demonic energy. While we have met some mercenary charlatans in the alternative health industry, most involved are genuinely interested in helping people whose pains and symptoms are not adequately dealt with by orthodox medical practice. What concerns us is that the Biblical answers for healing have been ignored or rejected.

There are nurses in training who will tell you that they are being taught how to wave their hands over clients lying on a bed, and to diagnose diseases that way. That is not the scientific method of diagnosis, but of divination. This is being taught today in some nursing training schools. We know nurses who will not attend certain classes because of the New Age/occult training given. Many nurses are speaking and writing now about bio-energy and Life Forces. This sounds very scientific, but these are occult. This is getting deep into our culture, it is even getting into normal medical practice now, and we need to be very careful.

If you are unsure what your doctor is doing to your body, ask him or her. You are paying, so you are entitled to know what they are doing to you. Some well-known doctors who have good medical qualifications have abandoned the whole area of scientific medical practise and gone into the alternative health area. The pull is often the money, because there is a lot of money in Alternative Health. Some recognize there is more than the physical and mental aspects which are usually all that orthodox medicine deals with. Quite a few have a fascination with the "paranormal." Some people are disillusioned, disturbed and they want something new and different.

Most Alternative Therapists are familiar with several types of other therapies; a chiropractor may use Applied Kinesiology or muscle testing. There is a cross-use of various therapies, whether occult-based or not. The problem for many people is that because it works they don't look any further. We need to ask "What makes it work?" A therapist may use iridology or foot reflexology. You have a migraine headache and you lie down and someone massages your foot. Your commonsense should tell you there is no connection. But he or she starts massaging your foot and your headache goes away, so you are healed. It's either a placebo effect, some form of trance hypnosis, or something has been massaged into your body.

Index Of Some Major Alternative Healing Therapies

Acupressure

Acupressure is basically only Acupuncture without needles. This laying-on of hands uses psychic energy based on the occult principles of the life-force or energy of Taoism.

Acupuncture

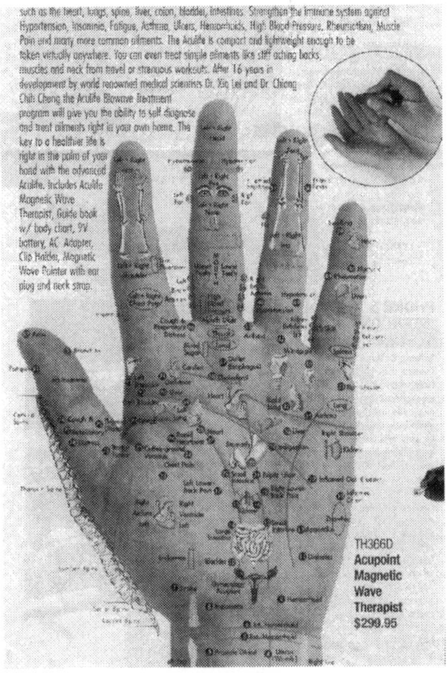

Acupuncture is a therapy originating in Taoism about 3000 BC in China. It is based on the belief that "energy" flows through our bodies, the earth and all the universe. This energy is not magnetic - it is psychic. Illnesses are claimed by most Alternative Health Therapists to be caused by blockages to these energy flows. It is claimed the way to remove the blockages is to insert acupuncture needles into particular parts of the body to stimulate them. These parts are claimed to be on lines or meridians (invisible channels of "vital energy") called Ch'i. These meridians have no relationship with nerves or blood vessels, and there is still no conclusive scientific reason why acupuncture should work, despite many years of research.

The picture claims to show which body parts may be healed by using Acupuncture on different parts of a hand. There is no physiological connection between the two.

Most writers who favor Acupuncture rely on cosmic, spiritist and occultic terms which they adorn with pseudo-scientific labels. They overestimate the ailments they claim they can cure, and most successes

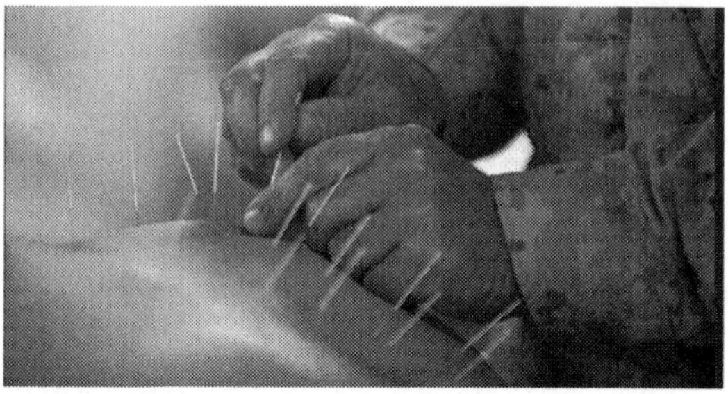

have a psychological basis. Placebos can explain much of the healing. *"A placebo is the term used to describe a medicine (or pill) given to a patient, not because it will have any definite action but because the patient will not be satisfied unless he (or she) receives some active treatment,"* according to Black's Medical Dictionary.

Controlled medical studies conclude that no organic diseases (e.g. infections, cancers and hereditary complaints) have ever been cured by acupuncture. Interestingly, many Acupuncturists claim they can induce mind changes and cure inner conflicts. As these problems are essentially spiritual or emotional in nature this raises further questions. Most practitioners use Traditional Chinese Medicine techniques which have an occult basis.

There is some evidence that Acupuncture can alleviate pain, and it has been claimed that this is the main reason people go for this treatment. Some forms of pain control using acupuncture could be explained on the basis of either stimulation of endorphin release; or the "Gate Control" theory of pain, i.e. where the pain is blocked out by the application of a second, less noxious, stimulus. This is similar to transcutaneous electrical nerve stimulus (***Tens***) which is an accepted form of pain relief, used especially with some cancer patients. Even if pain relief is proven this does not make acupuncture right in most cases. It seems that for treatment to be successful the patient must put their faith in the practitioner. On that basis Acupuncture appears to be a spiritual rather than a medical/scientific technique. Acupuncture needles have been known to cause infections and nerve damage, convulsions and punctured lungs when not cleaned or when misplaced.

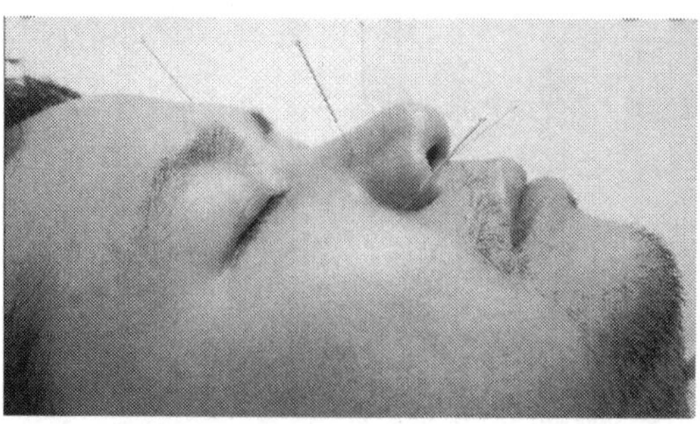

Moxibustion uses acupuncture needles while burning incense in the end protruding from the patient.

"Whether Acupuncture employs psychic (relating to the fallen human spirit) or spiritualist powers or both, one cannot be sure. We can be fairly certain, though, that it does not work through consistent and scientifically provable mechanisms and that there is every reason to suspect the involvement of occultic powers," according to Tony Bambridge, a British medical researcher. [7]

If a needle piercing the skin and going into the muscle tissue can bring about miraculous healing, there should be documented cases of healings also caused by piercing ears or standing on a tack. To date no such evidence has been offered. Because of the Taoist/pantheist basis, we believe the spiritual dangers of using acupuncture strong suggest it should be avoided in favour of safer alternatives. (Further scientific evidence may be found in "Acupuncture Diagnosed - Points of Contention," listed in the recommended reading.)

Acutouch

Significantly based on the same false premise as Acupuncture and Acupressure, Acutouch added electromagnetic and infrared waves, which practitioners still claim is based on Ch'i. The electronic circuitry focusing ch'i are hexagonal in shape because its Japanese "discoverer," Yamata Takoa, believed that a six-sided shape resonated ch'i more strongly. The real issue isn't using electromagnetic and infrared waves (which seem unproven as a therapy) but the use of the psychic force of ch'i (See Prana & Ch'i, page 31 onwards.)

Alexander Technique

Developed by Australian actor F. M. Alexander about a century ago, this technique aims to bring harmony to both mind and body. Ideal posture is to be visualized (conjured up in the mind) by the patient to help overcome physical strain caused by incorrect posture. Alexander claimed he was able to restore his stage voice by correcting his posture. Many people could lessen pain and strain on their bodies by better posture, and common sense will correct much of it.

Altered States of Consciousness

The human brain can be manipulated to such an extent that the brain's functioning, with respect to our sense organs, is brought to a neutral or zero condition. The person ceases to function actively and becomes semiconscious. At that stage the person's condition can be classified as being in an "Altered State of Consciousness." Hypnotism can do this, as can Meditation, Transcendental Meditation and other forms of Eastern meditation. Drugs can also do that, as can demon possession. Every Altered State of Consciousness is capable of exposing a person to the demonic realm. That is why most of these practices are dangerous. Some are psychological practices, some are physical manipulations (e.g., some massages by Chiropractors, Aromatherapists, etc.), and some are directly occultic.

Evidence from many Christian counselors shows that during the Altered State, the person's spirit and soul are loosened and separated, and what happens is that a demon or evil spirit comes in and locates within the soul and the spirit realm. It begins to give messages and cause bodily/physiological changes. The demon manipulates the mind, the mind begins to get messages from the spirit and that is how people operate, e.g. in trance state divination. That is why the Word of God is active and it separates between the soul and the spirit (see Hebrews 4:12) and gets at the demons and ejects them. Please note: this therapy has nothing to do with sedation or general anaesthesia for conventional surgical procedures, nor does it relate to going to sleep at night.

Anthroposophic Medicine

Rudolf Steiner (1861-1925) was the founder of Anthroposophy. This is a religious and philosophic belief system with strong occultic overtones. The part relating to health involves use of homeopathy, hydrotherapy, and special exercises. Although Steiner's teaching and methods have spread around much of the world, they are still strongest in mainland Europe, including his native Germany. Steiner took a holistic approach to life, having rejected Theosophy (despite being one of its leaders) and yet adopted much of it. Unfortunately he was involved in Spiritism and was unable to discern between good and evil spirits. Steiner sought to involve Spiritism in daily life, including medicine, diet, agriculture, (one television programme recently showed anthroposophic farmer burying cows horns stuffed with manure at full moon to aid productivity) architecture and education (Waldorf and Steiner Schools are the most well known). [8]

Applied Kinesiology/Muscle-testing

This therapy is a form of divination for the diagnosis of allergies. It was developed primarily for Chiropractors and Acupuncturists, by George Goodheart, a Chiropractor. If a person is thought to be allergic to, say, wheat flour, then the practitioner will put some wheat flour in the patient's outstretched hand. If the allergy is "proven," the arm will lose strength and may be forced to drop without much resistance and with only the slightest pressure. It is highly likely that most cases involve a form of hypnosis or suggestion, since the energy balancing claim has already been disproved. In addition to this psychic energy basis, because there is a serious danger of misdiagnosis, we recommend it be avoided.

Aromatherapy

Like so many other Alternative Therapists, most Aromatherapists view disease as a sign of imbalance between body, mind and spirit. One Magazine stated that "the (Aroma) Therapist may dowse a 'tally' from his patient, such as a lock of hair or a fingernail paring. This 'tally' will be placed in the centre of a dowsing disc. The swing of a pendulum suspended above it helps the aromatherapist decide which essential oils will restore his patient's inner balance most successfully, and then how best to apply them. Once taken, the 'tally' can be used any number of times to give a reading of which oils are necessary for any particular ailment." Dowsing is divination, or obtaining information from an evil spirit, and explained elsewhere why this is forbidden by God. (See Leviticus 20:6.)

Some Aromatherapists advertise that the use of essential oils "affect the physical and spiritual bodies through smell and absorption." Others wrote "Some experts (none were named) believe that essential oils contain the vital force and consciousness of the plant, and we experience the plant's energy as we inhale the vapours of the oils." They went on the state "The oils used in meditation enhance brainwave functions, and improve psychic and spiritual awakening." But hang on a minute here - no one has ever proved that a plant has a "Vital

Force," and as for claiming plant "consciousness," the dictionary describes this as "thoughts and feeling." We are curious to know of any research which demonstrates when a plant ever had a thought! If plants have feelings, how can any manifestation be proved? Do vegetables scream when harvested from the garden? What about when they are cooked and eaten? The reader can clearly see what a nonsense these claims by Aromatherapists (and some others) are when taken to their logical conclusion.

The Aromatherapists quoted above are admitting to a spiritual belief derived from occultic Buddhism and Spiritism, which no reputable medical scientist could accept. Certainly it involves a world-view totally contrary to Christian and Jewish belief.

Because psychic abilities bring us under God's judgement (see pages 23-30) it is not recommended we attempt to develop such abilities. Another word for psychic is medium - a person with the alleged ability to communicate with the spirit world. That issue is dealt with elsewhere in this book, and also in "Unmasking Spiritualism." (See back page) There is no spirit in a plant. It is merely a created object of vegetable matter which grows, produces seeds for its replacement, and then dies.

In a confusing and roundabout way Aromatherapists are admitting to channeling demonic or evil spirits into clients. We doubt their clients realise this, and suspect some of the Aromatherapists may not know it either.

Hospitals often have a rather "clinical" smell. Recent tests in British hospitals showed that where pleasant smells were released, there was a small but useful effect on anxious patients.[10] All smells, whether pleasant or otherwise, only have a brief effect. People who work in fish or meat processing plants do not notice the usual unpleasant smell after a few hours. This is due to adaptation by our noses' smell receptors. The odor may remain but it soon ceases to have any noticeable effect. The clinical effect of aromatherapy are only likely to last a few minutes, according to medical researchers. Let us not forget that some smells may aggravate Asthma or allergies.

In Animist cultures, healer priests use music and burning incense to produce trance states which allow spirits to enter to effect a cure. In Aromatherapy, the soothing massage, coupled with soft background music and sometimes accompanied by incense can produce the same trancelike effect, and is actually a form of hypnotism. Repetitive stroking of the forearm is a proven method of trance-inducement and Altered States of Consciousness.[11] We suggest that Aromatherapy may be used, with caution, provided it isn't by a "mixer" - someone using psychic components.

Auricular Therapy

This is based on the specialized use of Acupuncture solely in the ear. There are claimed to be over 200 points where needles inserted in the ear will bring relief and/or healing to body functions and diseases. Auricular Acupuncture is also claimed to heal such problems as migraine, asthma and arthritis. The major developer of this method was Dr. Paul Nogier, of Lyons in France. *"90% of Nogier's ear acupuncture zones are outside the only area of the ear which is fed by a branch of the (body's) autonomic system,"* according to medical researcher, Tony Bambridge.[12] This therapy has no anatomical basis and is not scientifically viable. Otherwise there should be verifiable reports of women of healing after having their ears pierced for decorative earrings or studs. The diagram shows the imagined points for ear acupuncture.

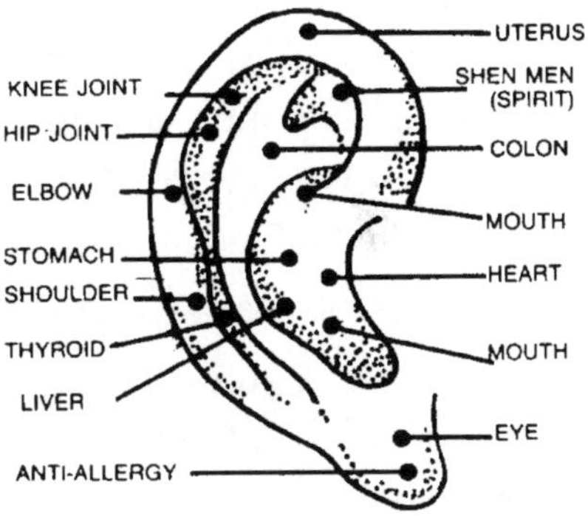

Ayurvedic Medicine

This is a Hindu-based therapy (developed about 2500BC) which uses yoga, altered sleep patterns, deep meditation, diet and massage, allegedly to stimulate the healing of the whole person - body, soul and spirit. Indian Occultist Dr. Deepak Chopra is probably the most well-known Ayurvedic proponent at present. There is a serious danger of misdiagnosis, and we cannot recommend its use because of the psychic/Prana energy involving evil spirits. (See entry for Yoga.)

Bach Flowers

This remedy is claimed to treat negative states of mind. Dr. Edward Bach (1886-1936) was a diviner, spiritist and Freemason, who held his hand over flowering plants to discover their unique healing properties.

This is a common practice by African herbalists to determine which plant to use for their cures. Bach floated the flowers on a bowl of water for several hours, with the claim the water had then been "potentized" or empowered with psychic energy in a similar way to homeopathy. Bach claimed that treating a patient's state of mind or moods will cause disease to leave. [13] (See Deuteronomy 18:9-14)

Bio-energetics

Described by some as a westernized form of yoga, Bio-energetics uses a combination of movements, breathing exercises and physiology in an attempt to overcome depression, lack of self-confidence and various anxieties. It was developed by American Alexander Lowen during the 1960's as an extension of Orgone Therapy.

Biofeedback - or Autogenic Training

This practice is an extended application of psychosomatic medicine, in that the mind controls the body. It is a mild form of self-hypnosis. It was developed by Elmer and Alyce Green. It uses electronic equipment to teach how to control brain waves that influence bodily function, and is mostly used in a search for higher levels of consciousness similar to the trances experienced by eastern gurus and holy men. It could be described as an electronic meditation technique to enable one to become one with the "Brahman, or Universal Soul." Recently there have been some trials using these techniques and equipment on paralyzed accident victims helping them retrain their muscles (with some success) and also on sufferers of stress-related ailments.

They are now claiming these machines can relieve inner stress and depression that fosters addiction. These are psychological and/or spiritual problems usually solved with proper counseling, rest, forgiveness and acceptance. Great care is needed in the use of these machines to ensure they are not used for occultic means. The effects and related issues are similar to those of hypnosis. (See Isaiah 47:9-15.) Many university students have also been unwittingly exposed to the effects of this physical therapy in the course of their psychology studies. Some therapists rely on meditation practices with an occultic basis, which can also involve Guided Imagery. Beware of "mixers" - those with a psychic basis.

Biorhythms

This is a predictive/interpretative pseudo-science, based on the belief that our biological clocks have cycles which significantly affect us. It is claimed we have three cycles;

an intellectual clock with a 33 day cycle,

an emotional clock with a 28 day cycle, and

a physical clock with a 23 days cycle.

Computerized analysis and charts are used to work out when a person may be more creative, or accident-prone. This is very similar to Astrology. (see Deuteronomy 4:19). Orthodox medicine rejects the predictive nature of this therapy.

Body Light

This self-awareness program is based on the concept that repression of the emotions and sexual energies lead to blockages in the "Life Force." It can include aspects of Gestalt Therapy, reflexology, polarity therapy, inner-child work, meditation, creative visualisation, art and dance therapies.

Bowen Technique

This therapy was developed by Australian Thomas Bowen during the 1950's. It is claimed to be *"a dynamic system of muscle and connective tissue movements that effectively yet gently realigns the body and balances and stimulates energy flow, empowering the body's own resources to heal itself. It is holistic and non-invasive..."* [14] This therapy is popular with Chiropractors, Osteopaths, Touch for Health instructors, natural therapists, massage practitioners and a few medical practitioners. But if there is no energy to balance, this therapy cannot work using recognized medical/scientific principles, but instead relies on a spiritual basis.

Channeling

Voluntary spirit-possession is probably the best explanation for this practice. A spirit enters the body and speaks as a spiritual "guide" to or through the person. Other

> **CHANNELLING**
>
> **THE PLEIDIAN CONNECTION**
> ANAKYA ORANA CHANNELLING
> XIAUD FROM THE PLEIADES
> **Share in discussionon Personal Transformation, spiritual insights and much more...**

> Hello,
> My name is XXX
> My role as a healer is to allow my guides to flow their energy through my physical body. This enables me to heal through the human energy field.
> With love and wisdom, my guides will work with you to promote health and bring your body into a state of balance and wellbeing.
> My technique includes:
> - Polarity
> - hands on healing to release blocks and refresh you physically, mentally, emotionally and spiritually
> - gentle spine adjustment
> - cranial therapy
>
> The above advertisement from a local newspaper admits that guides or demons work through this woman. There is no human energy field. She is deceived, & deceiving others

names for channelers include mediums, psychics, magicians, shamans, satanists and gurus. Many such occultists have admitted that these spirits have tricked, lied to or injured their hosts. *"Even doing their best to imitate good, these spirits appear to have a difficult time suppressing their desires to harm men,"* according to Ankerberg and Weldon. [15] These spirits are invited in by involvement in drug-taking, meditation, yoga, T.M., or hypnosis etc. Contact with these spirits has also come through seances and ouija boards.

Most of these spirits claim (falsely) to be the spirits of the human dead. Many claim to have lived several lifetimes and to have discovered the secrets of life and death, and want to produce a New Age of peace and harmony. Some mediums even claim to channel dolphins, fruit, vegetables and even computers from the future. Along with many scientific critics we suspect sanity could be an issue here. There is significant evidence that involvement in the occult does produce a very high proportion of mental patients.

Contrary to false and misleading statements these spirits are not "God's angels." True angels glorify Jesus Christ, give revelations which are Scriptural, and don't seek publicity for themselves. Channeled "angels" are the exact opposite. These are not "new powers of the mind," or some "higher self" or "intuition." The real and obvious motive of these "Spirit Guides" (which the Bible calls demons) is to inoculate people against a belief in Jesus Christ. *"The hidden purpose of the spirits is to gain the confidence of men (and women) so they can influence and control them, to bring their eventual spiritual ruin."* [15a]

Channelling has been associated with many religions, including Hinduism, Buddhism, Shinto, Islam, Animism, Eckankar, the Moonies,

Anthroposophy, Mormonism, Christian Science, the Lucis Trust, and Swedenborgism etc. Some prominent people influenced or used by spirit guides include Uri Geller, Edgar Cayce, Shirley MacLaine, Elisabeth Kubler-Ross, Ram Dass and other Hindu gurus, Rosemary Altea, Johnathon Edwards and many more.

Chiropractic

It must be stated that the authors have met several genuine Christian Chiropractors who refuse to utilize the occultic methods developed by the founder, D.D. Palmer, and used by many other members of their profession. We urge caution rather than avoidance of Chiropractors, for that reason. Chiropractic therapy should not be confused with Spinal Manipulative Therapy (SMT) which is used by Physiotherapists, some Chiropractors and many other orthodox medical specialists. SMT is generally safe and effective because it is based on treating musculoskeletal problems which cause headaches, back pain and pinched nerves etc. This is medically sound.

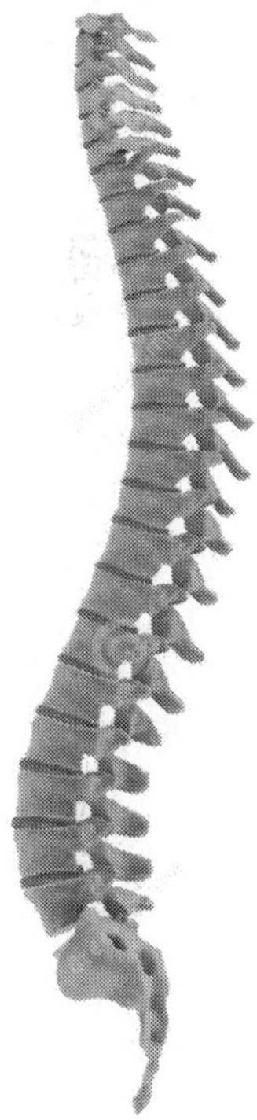

The human spine is made up of 26 bones which lock together to support the muscles and organs of the body

Founder/discoverer D.D. Palmer was a prominent spiritist, magnetic healer (hypnotist) and Phrenologist (he divined illnesses by feeling the bumps on a patient's head - long since rejected as a scientific method of diagnosis). However, popular and politically powerful in many countries, the occultic form of Chiropractic should correctly be called ***Chiromancy***, meaning 'divination by hands.' This term poses difficulties for Christian Chiropractors whose world-view, training and practice reject such occultism.

Palmer thought that diseases were caused by "Subluxations" of the spinal vertebrae. Medical subluxations are a partial dislocation of a joint, and a term sometimes applied to a sprain. Chiropractic Subluxations are not visible to X-rays, and are claimed to only be seen when the patient moves. Taking a legitimate medical term and changing its meaning has brought confusion which could have been avoided if Chiropractors had invented a different term. According to Dr. William T. Jarvis (Professor of Prevention Medicine at Loma Linda University, and also president of the US National Council Against Health Fraud) Chiropractors have never defined their version of subluxation in measurable terms, nor proven it exists. [16] Chiropractors aren't the only health professionals in the world, yet they are the only ones who believe chiropractic subluxations exist. This is a problem.

What Palmer explained is that the flow of "Innate Intelligence" or "energy" was being blocked and thereby affecting nearby organs. The basic chiropractic idea is that most diseases result from misaligned vertebrae which cause nerve pressure. The hand contact is as important as the spinal adjustment, which is interesting due to its origins in magnetic healing. This "laying on of hands" attempts to alter the electromagnetic or "Life Field" by removing harmful energy or adding beneficial energy. There is a psychic component often called an *Energy Transfer* from 'doctor' to patient. ***Innate*** is a basic Chiropractic concept which is described as a primal source of energy or ***Vital Force***, or as the founder of Chiropractic D. D. Palmer says, "Innate is that Intelligence which fills the universe." This is the impersonal force of Eastern and occult mysticism. One well-known New Zealand Chiropractor openly admits that his healing has a Hindu basis to it, using the Chakra system. Another said that most Chiropractors who don't start out with psychic abilities tend to develop them as they proceed with their training.

Chiropractors who operate exclusively in the area of spinal adjustment on a purely medical basis (and there is nothing wrong with that) are a small minority, understood to be about 10%. However there is one particular manipulation of the neck which involves a sudden twist which is incredibly dangerous, and which has caused stroke, death from the damage to the carotid arteries and paralysis by spinal cord damage. People should never subject themselves to this type of manipulation. There was a very public trial of a Canadian Chiropractor in 2003 where he was convicted of causing death using this very technique. Those who use ***Energy Healing, Muscle Tests*** (Applied Kinesiology) etc. should also be avoided. We personally know of several people who have required deliverance from a 'Spirit of Chiropractic' following involvement with a chiropractor, and significant improvement in their health followed. We have also heard of many others. If Traditional Chiropractic were completely medically/scientifically valid and Biblically sound this would not occur. Clearly it can be something else. Beware of "mixers" - those with a psychic basis.

Christian Science

Correctly known as ***"First Church of Christ, Scientist,"*** this religious cult was founded in Boston USA last century by Mary Baker Eddy. This group, whose teachings can be traced back to pantheistic Hinduism, believes that all disease is caused by sin, and the existence of matter is totally denied. Modern physics and better education in scientific subjects has seriously disproved this group's beliefs, resulting in less than ten percent of the former following remaining.

Color Therapy

Sometimes called ***Radiesthesia or Chromotherapy***, this is a spiritist method of diagnosis like using a ***Divining Rod or Pendulum***. Treatment can include the use of particular colors for healing, diets based on Zodiac charts of food, or even meditating on particular colors with incantations. Effective color healing requires occultic powers to observe the patient's AURA and noting the lack of specific colors which is claimed to indicate deficiencies in the flow of energy. There is no scientific basis to it - it is spiritism, sorcery or fraud.

According to Dr. Kurt Koch, Color Therapy is more prevalent in New Zealand than in any other country. [17] He even singled out one conservative Christian denomination for having most of the colour therapists in New Zealand. This is a denomination which claims that all spiritual gifts died out with the Apostles, (not widely held, this belief is called "Dispensationalism"), which they think means that any 'divine healing' must be demonically inspired. In their unbelief and legalism they have replaced the truth of the Bible with the very lie they claim they oppose. We must ask why demons could bring healing when, according to this thinking, God cannot? These people are somehow blinded. Color therapy should not be confused with using color for a pleasant house decor or dress sense.

Colonic Irrigation

Believing that toxins build up in the large bowel and that this buildup causes many health problems, Colonic Irrigation is a form of hydrotherapy. Water at body-temperature is pumped into the rectum, and when flushed out helps remove all waste material. Some Colonic Therapists claim they can also treat backache, bad breath, lung congestion, fatigue and indigestion through this therapy. There is a danger of infection in this process. Medical practitioners regard this therapy as dangerous, useless and an easy way to make money from the gullible.

Cosmic Energy

This is actually Psychic Energy. It is spiritual and involves the use of Satanic power. Two of the best known psychic energies are ***Prana*** (a Hindu/Yogic energy involving the potentially lethal rising of the spirit serpent ***Khundalini***), and ***Ch'i*** (the Taoist energy or "Life Force" claimed to flow through all the universe via meridians; this involves Yin and Yang, the opposing yet harmonizing forces of Taoism). These essential Vital Forces of Prana and Ch'i are based on the belief that the universe is God, and since we are part of the universe then we too must be part of this impersonal God. This power or energy derives exclusively from spiritual beings and since God forbids its use by human beings (See Deuteronomy 18:10-11 & others) it is reasonable to expect that it is not from God. Human beings do not have any such power inherent within them. (See pages 26 for further details.)

Crystals and Gem Healing

Crystals are claimed to transmit "Cosmic Energy" or "Vibrations." These are often used for psychic healing, to manipulate other people or even to induce pregnancy. Crystals are commonly used by New Age occultists. It is claimed that stagnant, heavy layers of electromagnetic energy accumulate from stress and emotional trauma; the patterning created is carried in the DNA at "soul level" and accompanies us through each incarnation or lifetime. (The Bible says we each live once and after death comes judgement, Hebrews 9:27.) Gems may also be immersed in water, which is then used to treat diseases. Amethysts may be worn for spiritual healing, while quartz is worn for physical healing.

Other Crystal healers use Bloodstone for physical; Lapis Lazuli for mental; Rose Quartz for emotional; and Apophyllite for spiritual

THE POWER OF CRYSTAL. CLOSE AT HAND

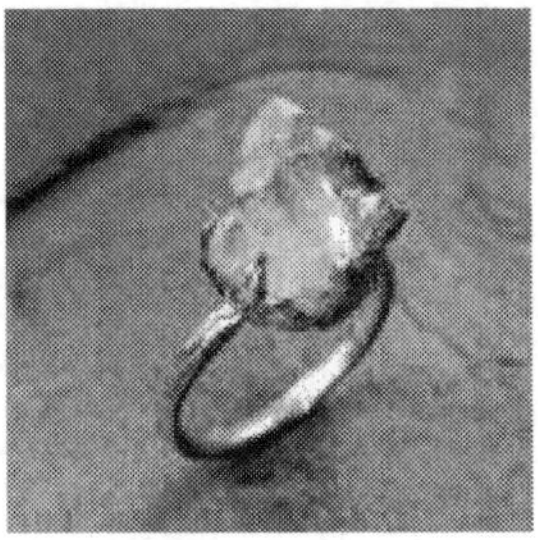

Experience The New Age in a dazzling ring, exclusively designed with pure energy. Radiating from the captivating quartz crystal ... aglow on your finger. Alive with the spirit of a New Age. Drawing power to you ... revitalising. Harmonising. Revealing your own inner glow of well-being. The Crystal Power Ring. Genuine quartz crystal set in a brilliant sculpture of 22 carat gold coated over sterling silver. Sparkling with a full-cut diamond. Style for The New Age. Now, you've got the power.

This advertisement from a local brochure describes occultic/spiritual power

healing. There is no evidence that crystals have any power of their own, despite the false claims otherwise.

Small crystals have been used in home-made radios for decades, but these can only receive sound and high frequency signals which are broadcast from a transmitter powered by batteries or mains power. The crystal simply separates different types of radio signals. Such signals and radio waves are all around us all of the time. The only proven power or energy from mineral rocks is extremely toxic to humans and all other physical life. These minerals include uranium, radium, plutonium and others used for nuclear purposes etc. The crystals claimed to bring healing and spirit communication are merely occultic charms in disguise through which people's lives can be influenced by the spirit realm.

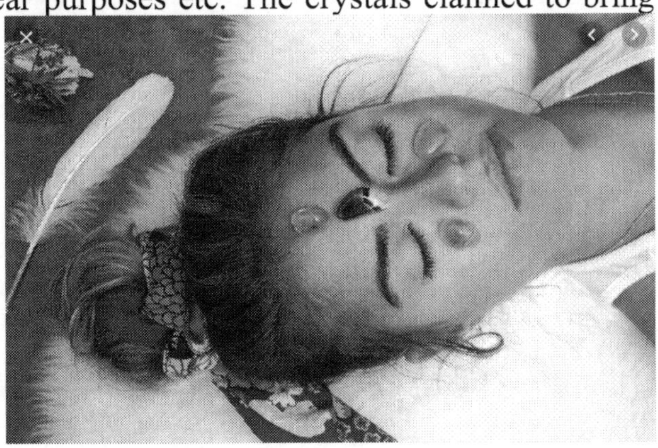

This photo shows the use of crystals in Reiki healing too.

Divination

Divination is the primary form of Fortune Telling, that is, seeking information about the future. Fortune Telling is one of the three major recognized branches of the Occult; the others are Spiritism (contact with the spirit world); and Magic (controlling or manipulating nature by commanding evil spirits). Divination is used widely in most Alternative Healing practices, including Homeopathy, Therapeutic Touch, Acutouch, Color Therapy, Applied Kinesiology, Bach Flowers, Reflexology, Acupuncture, Anthroposophic Medicine, Biorhythms and many more. Divination is knowledge obtained by Biblically-forbidden means, and should be repented of immediately. The source of the information is demonic. (See Deuteronomy 18:9-14, 1 Samuel 15:22-24, Acts 16:16-18, & others.)

Divining or Dowsing Rods are used for locating the place of the supposed energy imbalance, and are also used for locating water and other buried substances in the ground. These are usually Y shaped, with the two shorter arms held in the diviner's hands, and the stem moves until it points down to the water underground. Both dowsing rods and pendulums are operated by those who have psychic power, usually inherited from family members who were involved in sorcery. It is the person who has the power, not the rod or pendulum. That power is occult - evil supernaturally sourced, (See Hosea 4:10-14, Isaiah 47:11-15). (See pendulums also.)

Do-In

This is a combination of acupressure, exercise and massage, often practiced in Japan and China.

Dream Therapy

To be successful, this therapy requires spirit divination for analysis. Results are usually contradictory, unsubstantiated and of no long-term benefit. The authors warn against trusting evil spirits for healing, guidance and direction, (See Jeremiah 23:32).

Encounter Groups

This is a later development of the Human Potential Movement, where those involved are claimed to reach their real selves and feelings by techniques widely recognized by professionals as forms of brainwashing. Vulnerable participants are often harmed by this, and suffer guilt, rejection, self-doubt etc.

Enneagrams

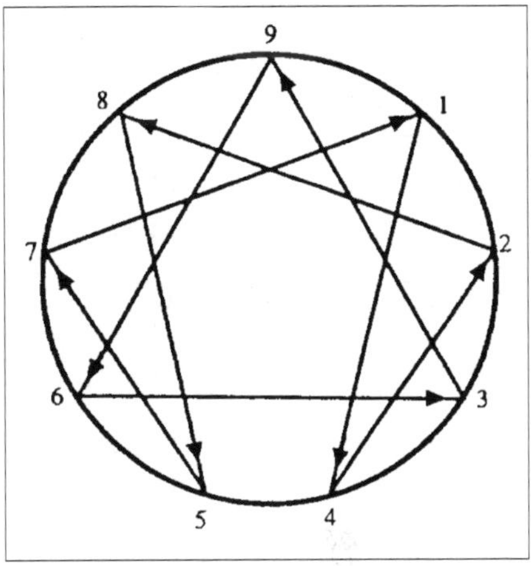

Ennea is Greek for nine, and gram refers to a line drawing. The Enneagram is a circle with nine points on its perimeter and two line drawings inside the circle connecting the nine points. (See the diagram.) Part of the significance of these lines comes from "mystical" numbers and the decimal point. The circle symbolizes "one" so the triangle gets meaning from splitting one by three, six and nine, resulting in the infinitely repeating numbers .3333..., .6666..., .9999.... The other figure derives from dividing one by the mystical seven, resulting in the "mysterious" number .142857142857... repeated to infinity, yet containing no multiples of three. Another part of the significance of the inner figures comes from arrows on the lines indicating the direction of least resistance within the system. By an Enneagram, most people mean a personality-typing system based on the diagram. Nine personality-types are placed on the nine points around the circle.

* One is a perfectionist, angry at the world's imperfection.

* Two is a proud helper who tries to fulfill everyone's needs.

* Three is a superficial deceiver living out roles.

* Four is a melancholic elitist among so many unsophisticated plebeians.

* Five observes the world, stingily absorbing knowledge without giving back to others.

* Six is a coward committed to law and order.

* Seven is a happy story teller who relishes every experience.

* Eight is power hungry and effective.

* Nine avoids conflict and seeks calm.

The arrows point out how the nine types improve or worsen. Becoming like the next type in the arrow's direction makes one more compulsive; becoming the next type against the arrow's direction frees one from compulsion.

Most Enneagram teachers claim that it is an ancient spiritual tradition from the Sufis (Islamic mystics) passed down by esoteric oral tradition and revealed to the West by G. I. Gurdjieff. Some claim it is 5,000 years old, while others say it is 2,000 years old. The antiquity claims to give the Enneagram its authority.

However, these claims to antiquity are nonsense, serving merely to create a myth or wisdom for a theory without scientific support. Sufism began in the 15th century so it could not be the source of an older tradition. Because the inner geometric figures connect the nine points with mystical numbers based on the decimal point invented in the 15th century, the Enneagram must have been concocted since then.

The earliest evidence about its origin comes from the turn of the 20th century, when Gurdjieff brought it from a Central Asian Sufi group. John Bennett, a Gurdjieff disciple, says the Enneagram had been used in numerological fortune-telling. Gurdjieff used it to describe nine stages of mystical enlightenment, but neither he nor his disciples mention personality typing. The explanation came from Dr. Claudio Naranjo, the Esalen psychologist who introduced the Enneagram to the United States in 1970. In a lecture taped in San Diego at the Association of Christian Therapists meeting held in February 1990, he said the system of nine personality types was invented in Chile by Ichazo.

Ichazo placed the "seven capital sins" on the numbers around the circle and added deceit to number three and cowardice to number six to fill in the gaps. Ichazo theorized that all personalties are centered on one vice, with the rest of one's distortions flowing from it. To this, Naranjo added a Freudian defence mechanism for each type and a short description of characteristics. He brought Esalen students to Chile for a workshop on the newly invented Enneagram of personalities and then taught it at Esalen.

Many questions about the Enneagram arise. Why believe Ichazo's theory that only nine personality types exist? Or that he has identified the correct nine? Why believe, as some claim, that capital sins plus deceit and cowardice are the cores of character structure? No psychological studies of these theories have been done, so they remain completely unproven. They have no supporting evidence, except the practitioner's anecdotes. [18]

Personality Typing of various kinds is often used by counsellors, whether in ignorance or knowledge of the occultic roots. The claims of personality typing are subjective, and fall far short of some counselors' boasts. Even if these systems were accurate in describing personality types (and most are not) they do little to bring healing, and actually provide an excuse not to seek change when it is necessary. Our true self-worth, healing and wholeness come from a personal relationship with Jesus Christ.

Faith Healing

Although it can often include the use of placebos, this is a mixture of false spiritual healing and mind control. The patients will themselves to be healed, despite the medical and other evidence. This can be extremely dangerous unless the sick person seeks professional medical assistance. A number who have used this method later die of serious illnesses because they chose to reject medical help and advice early enough, resulting in the disease or illness going beyond where the body and medical science could help. "Mind-over-Matter "techniques are usually deceiving. Pride and denial of sickness are the major factors. Sometimes it is the "Big boys don't cry," syndrome. One movement which has used this method widely is "Christian Science," which is neither Christian, nor scientific. It is also evident in a few Charismatic and Pentecostal groups who are described by other Christians as the "Hyperfaith" movement.

Feldenkrais Method

Substantially used by sports people as a form of body psychotherapy, this is a combination of exercises, including stretches, Yoga and the Alexander Technique. Moshe Feldenkrais, an Israeli physicist, developed what is sometimes referred to as "Western Yoga," after he suffered a knee injury and spent two years studying Yoga. His method is also known as ***Functional Integration,*** which can involve up to one thousand physical and meditation exercises. Feldenkrais claimed to discover that having once experienced a movement, we could achieve greater results through the use of our imagination rather than repeat the exercise.

Flotation Therapy

The patient is immersed in a dark, warm, soundless water chamber, and the method involves sensory deprivation. Depending on the emotional and mental state of the patient, it can be relaxing, or bring total panic. Expert supervision is essential, but the emotional and mental risks outweigh any potential benefits.

Geopathic Therapy

This is a philosophic/religious belief that the Earth's magnetic field concentrates 'energy' into what are called "Ley Lines." It is claimed these lines can bring healing and also produce disease. Special instruments are claimed to detect excess energies, which can be balanced by moving your furniture or your house, if they are in "the wrong place."

Gestalt Therapy

A self-awareness programme (rather than a treatment), this is a "here and now," approach to feeling and thoughts related to the Human Potential Movement. It teaches people to live for the moment, and was developed by Frederick (Fritz) Perls (1893-1970) a German psychoanalyst.

Herbalism

This is the oldest and most widespread therapy. Plants have been the source of healing for millennia. These are generally good to have and are widely available. Herbal remedies, used as simple herbs, do have God-given healing properties. Ezekiel 47:12 speaks of leaves of healing for example. The dangers begin when formulae are given by divination, or charms and incantations are spoken over the herbs in their collection or processing. There is no such thing as a cure-all plant/natural remedy, despite claims to the contrary about plant products such as Ginseng or Aloe Vera.

Not all herbs are good for us. As the use of herbs increases around the world, so also there has been an increase of medical problems, according to reputable medical research. Some reports sound warnings about herbal tea blends which can have more serious effects than the caffeine in regular teas which people are attempting to avoid. Some herbs used in tea blends contain toxins and hallucinogens, and can bring about sickness because of their chemical clash. Some herbs are also addictive, and these should be used with care, or avoided. Careful research prior to use is highly recommended. Make sure you find out about the properties of the herbs you want to use before you go try them. Beware of "mixers" - those with a psychic basis.

Holistic Pulsing

This therapy involves a very gentle rocking at a rate of 120 to 160 beats per minute, the same as the foetal heart rate. This is claimed to create a safe and soothing environment for body, mind and spirit to heal. Emotional healing and self-acceptance appear to be the main goals.

Homeopathy

The English spelling is Homoeopathy, but the American spelling without the extra "o" is catching on. Homeopathy is one of the most popular and widely used of the Alternative Health Therapies and if users were asked what it is and why it works, a wide variety of answers would result. Most don't know. The vast majority think it is simply minced up herbs put into some sort of tincture and applied or used in a pill form. One of the biggest myths about Homeopathy is that it is a form of Herbalism. It is not. Minerals are often used, such as sulphur, phosphorus, potassium and the highly poisonous arsenic trioxide. Animal products are also used, such as the ink from Cuttlefish and the venom of the Bushmaster snake to name just two. However vegetable matter does form the basis for many Homeopathic remedies in the early stages of preparation. There are certain fundamental premises to Homeopathy, including the following:

The Law of Similars - like cures like - This means that a substance which would produce symptoms in a healthy person can cure those symptoms in a sick person. The disease is cured by the remedy that would cause the symptoms of that disease should it be given to a healthy person. This is ambiguous. Surely, we would not give someone with diarrhoea something which induces diarrhoea in a healthy person. They would never get out of the toilet!

The Law of Minimum Dose - This causes a scientific and mathematical difficulty of major proportions. Basically Homeopaths are saying that the more you water it down, the stronger is its ability to bring healing. Scientifically that is a nonsense, as has been pointed out by many authorities. If someone needs two painkillers of a particular dose, then giving them only half a tablet will not sufficiently ease their pain. An Australian Government Committee report said of this dilution in Homeopathy: *"There is not one example in the whole area of Pharmacology in which the simple dilution of a drug enhances the response it produces, any more than diluting a dye will produce a deeper hue, or adding less sugar will make food sweeter. "* [19]

What actually happens during the production of a Homeopathy remedy? Well, basically one part of the substance, whether it is snake poison, the head of a particular flowering herb or whatever, is added to nine parts of a neutral base such as water or alcohol which is then shaken by hand. Then one part of that mixture is taken and added to nine parts of the neutral base again, then shaken by hand again. The second dilution equals 1/100th. The third done the same way is 1/1,000th. The 4th is 1/10,000th, the 6th is 1/1,000,000th. It is able to be proven without question that at about the 24th dilution the molecules of the original substance are so spread through dilution there is less than one molecule per bottle. Scientifically there is no benefit from the herbal content above 6X. Let us give you some illustrations of the dilutions used in Homeopathy.

A Comparative study of Homeopathic Dilution

1 part in 40 is equivalent to the amount of sugar in a mug of tea or coffee if 1 teaspoon of sugar is added.

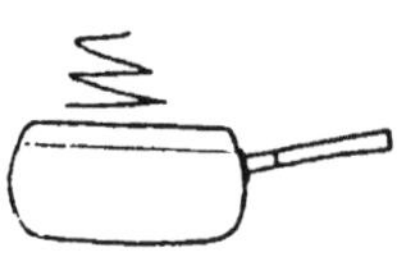

1 part in 150 is equivalent to the amount of salt in a saucepan of water (750 mls, or 1.25 pints) when 1 teaspoon of salt is added.

1 part in 1,000 is equivalent to 3X homeopathically. 1 part in 1,000,000 is equivalent to 6X homeopathically. This is equivalent to the dilution of 1 pinch of salt in a full (204 litres or 45 gal.) bath of water.

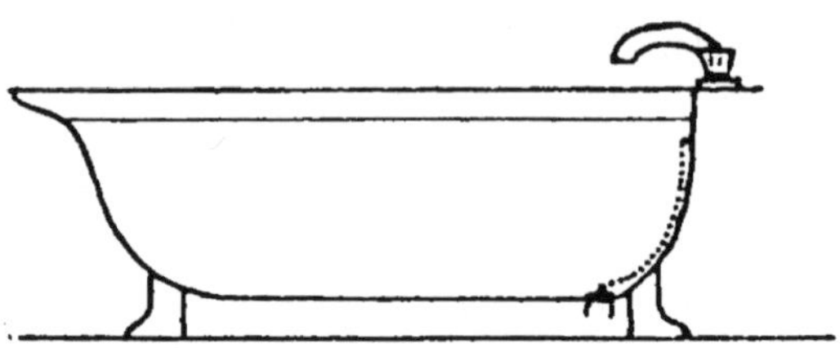

1 part in 1,000,000,000,000,000,000,000,000 is equivalent to 24X or 12C homeopathically. This is so diluted it does not register.

In order to visualize further the enormity of even the medium dilutions used in homeopathy it may be useful to realize that the homeopathic remedy dilution 12c (10^{24}) is roughly equivalent to depositing one pinch of salt in a volume of water the size of the Atlantic Ocean. This calculation is based on the assumption that this ocean is approximately 81 million square kilometres in size, and has an average depth of 3,700 metres. Truly a drop in the ocean!

Medical research has proved that homeopathic remedies bear no resemblance in their effects when compared to vaccine inoculations. That means there must be another reason why they work; yes, you guessed it - the hand shaking of the mixture is claimed to release dynamic energies, a ***Cosmic Vital Force***. In Psychic Healing this is transmitted through the laying on of hands, but through Homeopathy the hands are laid on the remedy and conveyed indirectly. Whether some admit it or not most Homeopathic remedies have a strong spiritual basis and bring occultic healing coupled with spiritual bondages.

The founder, Samuel Hahnemann, was a follower of Confucius, and deeply involved in occultic and Eastern philosophy and Freemasonry. Hahnemann did a test upon himself which resulted as much as any other event in the birth of homeopathy. *"Hahnemann decided to test the result of the quinine (Cinchona bark) on himself using the tincture. Although perfectly healthy at the time, within hours he developed the symptoms of a malaria-like illness with intermittent fever, chilly extremities, prostration, drowsiness and flushed cheeks. These symptoms disappeared as soon as he ceased taking quinine."*[8] Hahnemann's experiment has been criticized by others, who, having attempted to repeat his experiment, did not obtain the same results. They abandoned further investigations and subsequently condemned a practice which was so different to normal medical treatment. Hahnemann apparently had a particular sensitivity to quinine which is quite rare. Hahnemann's experimentation with quinine shows the man was deluded enough to believe that his reaction (which he misinterpreted as malaria) was somehow an explanation that a substance that could induce an illness could also cure it. Scientifically these medicines are so diluted they are safe, however the spiritual danger seems more significant and Homeopathy should be avoided. *(Recommended additional reading "Homeopathy Diagnosed - Powerful Water" & "Homoeopathy - Some things aren't what they seem." both available from Jubilee Resources.)*

Hypnosis/Hypnotherapy

Hypnosis means being put in an artificial state of sleep or trance, or a reduced or Altered State of Consciousness. It is about giving up control of one's mind and will to someone else, someone who may have different values and beliefs from you. The person being hypnotized has no power to select or prevent anything the hypnotist suggests while in the trance state. It is possible to be hypnotised against your knowledge or will. It eliminates will power and the conscious use of the senses. Self hypnosis is among the most dangerous forms due to people not really knowing what they are doing. Trance states can be induced by

1. Staring at something such as a bright light, or swinging pendulum etc.
2. Rhythmic drum beating or some other music
3. Regular and continuous stroking of the skin
4. Rhythmic breathing
5. Incense or other strong aroma
6. Some relaxation exercises.

Hypnosis is largely based on the teachings of Franz Mesmer, from whose name we get "mesmerism" - an early name for this practice. Opinions on hypnosis differ widely even among experts. Dr. Paul Tournier of Geneva is opposed to it because he sees it as an attack on the human psyche (the soul or spirit). Others would use it for diagnosis but not for therapy. Among Christians there is wide agreement that hypnosis opens the way for evil spirits, according to Roy Livesey, a former Alternative Therapist and now Christian. Writer Emile Kremer sees hypnosis as an oriental art of suggestion which binds the patient's spirit with occultic powers. [20]

The use of hypnosis for therapy seems very questionable to almost all Christian experts that we have researched. Wilson and Weldon state their mistrust of hypnosis due to its similarity to mediumistic trance states, its occultic use in Yoga and spiritualism, its similarity to the Biblically-forbidden practice of charming and that the will must be surrendered to another person. They concluded that it was impossible to say that hypnosis is a generally safe practice when so little is known of the mind and the spirit world. Wilson and Weldon recommend that hypnosis be avoided. [21]

In view of such strong statements expressed by reliable experts in their fields hypnosis seems better left alone. Dr. Kurt Koch mentions cases where hypnotic trances, sometimes lasting days on end, could only be broken by prayer in the name of Jesus Christ.[22] The inescapable conclusion is that there is a darker spiritual basis to hypnosis.

One of the newer forms of hypnosis is ***Neuro Linguistic Programing*** (NLP), founded by Bandler & Grinder who adapted the teaching of hypnotist Milton Ericson. The primary purpose of NLP involves influencing or manipulating other people's decision-making without them knowing it. Even though this is taught in some Christian churches and counselling courses (some are called "Influencing with Integrity") it is ethically immoral and spiritually dangerous. This newspaper advertisement shows there is good money to be made (almost $3 per minute plus tax) despite the obvious dangers to clients.

AUTOMATIC HELP

ON-LINE PROCESSERS FOR SMOKING, SLIMMING, STRESS, SELF HYPNOSIS, SELF IMPROVEMENT

24 HRS **CALL** 7 Days

CLINICAL HYPNOTHERAPIST

HYPNOTIC NLP MIND LINE

Calls cost $2-95 per min + gst

Free after 1st 15 min. No Children

I CAN HELP YOU TO HELP YOU

Another newer branch of hypnosis is PSH - ***Private Subconscious-mind Healing*** - which claims to be about 'healing the feeling.' PSH is claimed to help people overcome compulsive habits including smoking, overeating, gambling etc., anxiety, self-esteem, confidence problems, stress and memory problems, phobias, depression, psychosomatic conditions and all with permanent transforming solutions. That is a big claim without proof. The authors have observed that hypnosis seems to be the tool of choice of counselors who lack any relationship with Jesus Christ. We cannot recommend Hypnosis.

Iridology

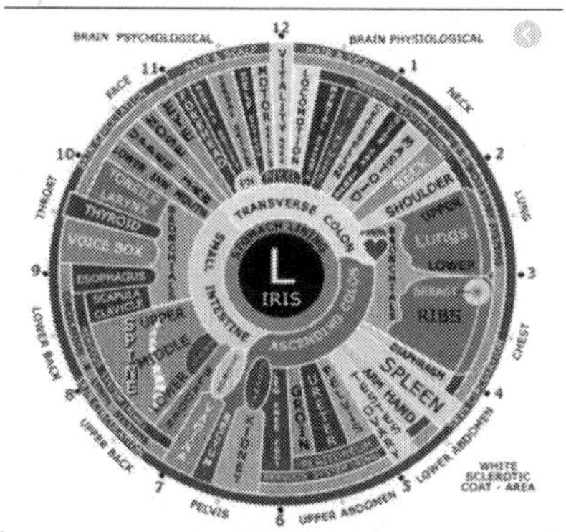

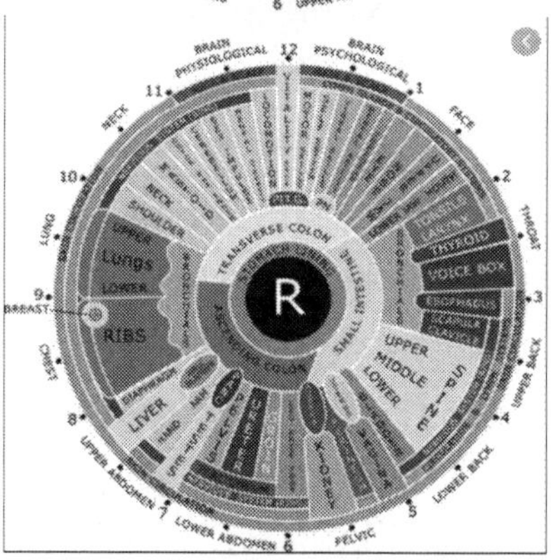

This is a method seeking to diagnose diseases in a person's body by observing the eyes, and particularly the iris. It was developed from an ancient occultic art by Ignatz von Peczely (1822-1911). Originally the eye was claimed to have only five zones, but this was increased to twelve to accommodate astrological divination. By looking at a person's iris, the practitioner attempts to see diseases in body organs. Studies by one of the authors uncovered not one but 19 different Iridology charts, so it appears to make some difference which practitioner a person goes to as to which disease is diagnosed. The danger of misdiagnosis is too serious and too common.

A recent controlled medical study designed to give Iridology practitioners an opportunity to prove their claims was very conclusive; they correctly diagnosed only 18 out of 762 patients - less than 3% correct. [23] Why would anyone who was sick risk going to an Iridologist with such a low chance of success? We don't recommend it, but one might have a better chance of diagnosing yourself with a household medical book. Eye fibres are not generally visible in those with brown eyes, such as Pacific Island and New Zealand Polynesians, Australian Aborigines, Africans, Asians and many who live around the Mediterranean Sea. Iridology is a mixture of divination and guesswork and is best avoided for your health's sake. It has nothing in common with eye examinations by medical doctors, etc.

Kinergy

Utilizing kinesiology to locate imbalances in the body's claimed energy field, healing and balance are claimed to be restored through the use of 'healing energy' (a spirit) or crystals. Kinergy is also claimed to bring healing to emotional as well as physical health problems.

Kirlian Diagnosis

This is not a therapy, but is claimed to be a diagnostic tool. Semyon and Valentina Kirlian were Russian radiologists who, in 1939, found they could capture on a photographic plate what was claimed to be the "bio-energetic field of living objects." The usual method used in diagnosis is the hand of a patient being placed on a sensitive photographic plate, through which a high voltage high-frequency electric charge is passed.

The resulting image shows an halo of light around the outline of the hand. Some claim this is an aura (or the astral body or our higher/psychic self) while others claim it is the energy being emitted from the body. If there does exist any energies or electricity inside our bodies, it is too weak to provide healing power to others. As Ankerberg and Weldon point out, *"If everyone has an inner core of mystical divine power, then everyone should be able to develop psychic powers. But in fact the only ones who do so are occultists who have spirit guides."*[24]

Kirlian therapists consult charts and analyze patterns formed to diagnose whether a health problem is emotional or physical, and then they could recommend a flower essence, a herbal medicine or hypnotherapy treatment. Kirlian photography has yet to receive any scientific validity, and one alternative authority admits that it isn't used very much any more because of the high cost and also *"because it proved not to be particularly reliable."*[25]

It needs to be pointed out that Kirlian photography also reveal aura-type images around inanimate objects such as coins, so it can't be a so-called "natural energy." Since we can't apply a spiritual meaning to these auras around inanimate objects, we shouldn't seek to apply spiritual meaning to similar auras claimed around living things by psychics and spiritists.

Lymphatic Drainage

This is a massage of the head and neck which is then claimed to boost energy levels and the immune system. The massage is then claimed to assist with detoxifying the body from alcohol and tobacco products, and heal recurrent colds, sore throats, fluid retention, constipation, chronic fatigue syndrome and much more.

Macrobiotics

Application of Taoist philosophy regarding positive and negative energies in food is the basis of this therapy. Yang food (including meat, eggs, spices etc.) is claimed to encourage aggressive behavior, tension and stress; while Yin food (including dairy products) is claimed to cause lethargy and depression.

Magnetic Therapy

The imbalances of our physical and spiritual make-up are claimed to be corrected through the use of magnets. No explanation seems possible as to how our spiritual condition could be so affected by wearing a magnetic bracelet or other jewellery, magnetic belts for knees, ankles, elbows or wrist joints. There are now even magnetic patches. The electrical appliances and other gadgets in our homes and work places do emit small amounts of electromagnetic field, but the primary indication in terms of health so far is the possibility of slightly higher cancer rate. There is no proven connection with our spiritual make-up.

Martial Arts

As this is sometimes treated in the West as a health and exercise regime, it has been included here. There are two main schools; one Buddhist, the other Taoist. Each move is designed to be uninterrupted and flowing so the end of one action is the beginning of the next, thus balancing the ***Yin and Yang***. ***Karate*** means "empty hand" and its primary purpose is to unite mind, body and spirit to achieve the unity envisioned by Zen Buddhism. ***T'ai Ch'i's*** stated ultimate goal is for one to become immortal by placing the body in harmony with nature, which will help one merge with the ***Universal Consciousness***. It is martial arts in slow motion. ***Aikido*** is a Japanese version of T'ai Ch'i, and means "the road to a union with the Universal Spirit," - a Buddhist concept. The power of Ch'i is claimed to be inhaled into the abdomen and exhaled through the hands. ***Kung Fu*** also claims its source of power from the psychic Ch'i, while ***Judo*** is ***Jujitsu*** without the killing aspect. According to their "Masters" martial arts can only be learned correctly with Buddhist, Taoist or Hindu meditation. *(See book "Insights into Martial Arts, Tai Ch'i, TM & Yoga" on back pages for more details.)*

Meditation

Everyone needs to be quiet and reflective at times, especially in such a busy world. The more stressful a person's life, the greater the need to take time out for rest and recreation. These could help explain the increasing popularity of various types of meditation. Most meditation today is for the promotion of particular spiritual groups, including the enhancing of the finances of such groups. Here are the names of some such groups; Ananda Marga Meditation and Yoga centre, Initiative Sciences, Buddha Dahrma Meditation, Friends of the Western Buddhist Order, Maharishi Health Education, Wholistic Meditation, Raja Yoga, Sri Chinmoy Meditation, Brahma Kumaris Raja Yoga, etc. The vast majority of these groups have obvious links with either Hinduism or Buddhism.

One meditation teacher claimed that meditation is *"a deliberate holding back of the conscious mind and emotions,"* and said *"This process of relaxing the body and shifting the mind into an alpha state allows you to go quietly within to balance yourself in a calm centeredness permitting the mind to recognize and have dialogue with the highest source of our facilities..."* [26] Since no proof has yet been provided that there exists any such energy to balance, this is either nonsense, self-worship, or communications with spiritual beings which the Bible calls demons. The Bible tells us to meditate on God's word, the Bible. We are not to empty our minds (due to the spiritual dangers involved) but we are to focus on the powerful promises in God's word, and the magnitude of His love and mercy for each of us.

Naturopathy

This usually involves diet, fasting and exercise, and sometimes herbal usage, which in themselves are good for all of us. However we have only met three naturopaths who are not also involved with iridology, homeopathy or several other occultic healing practices involving divination. This isn't so surprising when their own literature says they train in "herbal medicine, iridology, homeopathy, counseling and body therapies." A serious illness could be overlooked by a naturopath, thereby losing valuable time for the effective medical treatment. Common sense should show each of us how to work out our exercise and diet programmes without the detrimental spiritual additions. Shop around for those few genuine Naturopaths, as they can be most helpful without the occultic additions. Beware of "mixers" - those with a psychic basis. That will be most Naturopaths in our experience.

Necromancy

The most common methods of necromancy are through Ouija Boards, Seances, prayers and speaking to the dead. This occurs when a human being seeks the spirits of the dead in order to obtain information about the future. The Bible expressly forbids prayers directed toward anyone but God. That also means that prayers addressed to dead ancestors and "saints," are necromancy. (See Leviticus 20:27, & Isaiah 8:19).

Omens

These can appear either good or bad, but their use is forbidden in the Bible. African witchdoctors throw sticks and Cowry shells into the air and seek to divine or interpret their configurations when they land. Ancient Romans and Greeks checked the entrails (internal organs) of a chicken or animal which had been sacrificed (See Leviticus 19:26).

Orgone or Reichian Therapy

Developed by Wilhelm Reich (1897-1957) who claimed that sitting in a specially designed box would balance the patient's "energy flow," this is another therapy which deals with the blockage of "energies" which can cause stress, especially emotional. Reich also believed that most illnesses are caused by the inability to achieve orgasmic/sexual satisfaction. Reich's ***"Orgone Energy"*** is claimed to be the same as the universal Life Energy of Prana and Ch'i. Aspects of this theory have been used in "Bio-energetics," although these ideas have since been largely disproved and discarded.

Osteopathy

We have been reluctant to add this subject as it is probably one of the fringe practices most acceptable to the medical profession. Some osteopaths now have recognized medical degrees. However many of its practitioners hold similar beliefs to Chiropractors about energy healing, have involved some aspects of radiesthesia, acupuncture and homeopathy, and are organizationally attached to Naturopaths in New Zealand. Osteopathy is outlawed in some countries such as Belgium.

Osteopathy was developed by Andrew Taylor (1828-1917) and is the treatment of disease by the manipulation of bones (especially the spine) and muscles, their deformity being the supposed cause. Osteopathic "lesions" (which closely parallel chiropractic subluxations) cannot be scientifically demonstrated. Osteopaths have admitted this.[27]

Andrew Still often displayed his psychic powers to foretell events and even claimed to see beneath the patients' skin like an x-ray. He claimed to heal such illnesses as measles, diphtheria, eczema, pneumonia, T.B., mumps and gallstones. Since most of these are bacterial or viral infections with no scientific connection to manipulating the spinal column, today's Osteopaths seldom attempt such methods.

Although some osteopaths practice occultic healing it does not mean that all do, so we recommend you prayerfully shop around. Some of the medical panel this book was submitted to felt strongly to recommend all osteopaths be avoided, mainly because of the number of patients who have required spiritual counseling following osteopathic treatment. The orthodox medical profession does have a shortage of spinal specialists, which is part of the problem. There is one particular manipulation of the neck which involves a sudden twist which is incredibly dangerous, and which has caused strokes, death from the damage to the carotid arteries and paralysis by spinal cord damage. People should never subject themselves to this type of manipulation. Beware of "mixers" - those with a psychic basis.

Ouija Boards

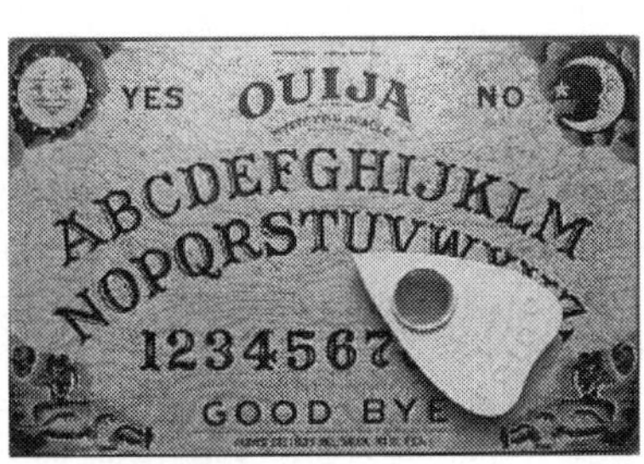

Ouija used to be known as "The Spirit of the Glass," although now there are non-glass versions available. Some manufacturers honestly state in their advertizing that its purpose is to communicate with the spirit world. Many people mistakenly think this is just a board game for fun, not realising its spiritual purpose. Our research shows that playing this "game" of Ouija Boards is virtually guaranteed to produce demonic oppression or even possession. Many people have gone into trances for several days, until a competent Christian came and broke the demonic power involved, with dramatic results (See Leviticus 19:31).[28] Many gullible Christians in North America have been using an "Angel Board," which is just an Ouija board relabeled. We have to question their lack of knowledge of the Bible, as well as their lack of discernment.

Palm Reading

Sometimes known as palmistry, this is occasionally used for the diagnosis of health problems, but more often claimed as a 'game' to disclose the future of a person. It involves interpreting the lines on a hand. This is one of the more highly developed methods of divination (See Micah 5:12).

Pendulums

These are usually metal, pointed, and suspended by a thread over the body or a chart. Magnetism is not involved but the point stops or circles over the affected area in healing methods. Non-healing uses include divining for mineral deposits and water. Both dowsing rods and pendulums are operated by those who have psychic power, usually inherited from family members who were involved in sorcery. It is the person who has the power, not the rod or pendulum. That power is occult - evil supernaturally sourced, (see Hosea 4:10-14, Isaiah 47:11-15).

Polarity Therapy

This is another therapy claiming to "Balance Energies," this one was developed by Randolph Stone (1890-1981) a man who claimed qualifications in three occult healing arts. It is claimed that polarity relationships between different parts of the body are brought into balance through a systematic usage of massage, manipulation, relaxation techniques, diet and exercise. The reality is that virtually anyone would feel much better through such stress-relieving activities despite the spiritual basis to this. The energy referred to is occult.

Primal Therapy

This practice is used mostly in humanistic psychotherapy and encounter groups, and was developed by Arthur Janor. Patients are usually hypnotized and encouraged to go back in their memories (including any "repressed memories") and relive their experiences. This could include regressing to birth, and it has been claimed patients can go back into the womb or even earlier lives. Screaming is normal. This practice is very dangerous, and in the longer term creates more problems than it claims to solve. If a person was mistreated or abused as a child, reliving the memory (real or imagined) doesn't actually relieve the pain, but tends to magnify it.

A few Christians use a non-biblical technique involving regression into a mother's womb and various developmental stages. This type of therapy is sometimes but erroneously called ***"Inner Healing."*** These are similar to what the prophet Jeremiah calls "False Visions, divinations, idolatries and delusions of their minds," (Jeremiah 14:14-16). This form uses Jesus as a spirit guide, which is very wrong. What is most needed with cases involving such abuse, etc., is expert counseling leading to forgiveness and compassion. (See Visualisation.)

Psychic Healing

This is merely another term for mediumship, or traditional witchcraft. Some psychic healers talk about balancing energy fields, but more often they use "spiritual" healing, in other words using or being manipulated by a familiar spirit. These bodiless creatures may sometimes be called "teacher," or "master," or "spirit guide," etc.

Psychometry is foretelling a person's future while holding an object belonging to that person. This form of divination is widely practiced in Spiritualist Churches.

Pyramid Power

Pyramids are claimed to concentrate healing and preservative powers. EEG experiments show that people sitting inside pyramids experience a similarity of brain activity to people in occultic meditation. This is Pyramid Healing, where the patient is made to sit under the pyramid, believing that pyramids tend

to concentrate healing "energy" into people. The practitioner is actually invoking demonic energy. When you come out of this pyramid you will feel different. Something has been put into you. Friends who have used this practice in the past and have since repented, have told us that "it fries your brain," and effectively disorientates a person. Media reports of a man in Auckland, New Zealand, who killed several members of his own family for no apparent reason said that he was a pyramid sitter. One medical authority we consulted suggested this man may have already been mentally unbalanced, and that sitting under the pyramid was a symptom and not necessarily a cause of what he did. Whatever the case, it does suggest there is more to sitting under a pyramid than meets the eye. Those who wish to remain sane and emotionally balanced should avoid sitting in pyramids.

Psionic Medicine

This is a divination-type diagnosis using a pendulum or dowsing rod to locate any causes of the body's inability to heal itself. Treatment usually involves homeopathy or naturopathy.

Psychic Surgery

In the main this is clever trickery aimed at convincing onlookers that the Shaman or witchdoctor has put his hand inside a patient's body and then removed organs, growths and diseased tissue. Examples of this quackery have been on television, especially from the Philippines and Brazil. Putting aside the drama of the event, sometimes the media teams had the blood and tissues tested later, with lab results proving the blood and organs came from chickens. In parts of Africa and Brazil, Psychic Surgeons using black magic have "removed" stones, knives and other non-living matter from desperate clients. There are also a few instances of psychic surgery which cannot be explained as trickery, and which are clearly supernatural.

Qigong

Qi is one of the Chinese terms for "Ch'i" and "gong" simply means "to be skilful at." These mainly involve a variety of moving or non-moving exercises in five main schools; Buddhist, Taoist, Confucianist, Martial and Medical Qigong. The mind and the body are to be regulated through relaxation and concentration of our mental and physical powers. Tai Ch'i and other martial art exercises are aspects of Qigong.

Radiesthesia or Radionics

This is based on the belief that a small electrical machine can emit special "Natural Life-healing Energies" for one particular patient only, regardless of the distance from the machine - sometimes called an "Abrams Box." It is claimed the patient may be diagnosed simply from an object they own and a life history. A patient may be unaware this is being done for them by a friend or family member. The machine or box has no power at all; the therapist is a channel for this psychic power. It is even admitted by users that the box will not work without a dowsing pendulum.[29] This form of energy healing was invented by Abbe Mermet, a Swiss priest, during the 1920's. Medical and scientific experts totally reject this method as quackery. If it does work, spiritism/ divination can be the only explanation why. Avoidance is highly recommended. (In Ezekiel 13:17-23, witches make their contacts with the souls of needy people through the use of charms - clearly a parallel.)

Rebirthing

This method seeks to discover problems arising from the time in the womb using deep-breathing and hypnotic age regression (and sometimes psychedelic drugs like LSD) to simulate the birth experience. Rebirthing is described by some as "Yoga for the West." Somewhat like Jungian depth analysis, it is closely related to Paramahansa Yogananda's Kriya Yoga. The experience has been described by one former leading practitioner as "like peeling off layers of consciousness much like peeling an onion, to eventually get to the core of one's being and reach the coveted state of Self-realization as a god." Practitioners often speak of "soul-retrieval" and "Past-life Regression," both of which are humanly impossible to do. The more rebirthing is practiced, the deeper the confusion and spirit/demon domination. Most who stop practicing say they suffer emotional drain and mental fog for years.

Reflexology

This is the same as acupuncture without needles, and uses PRESSURE POINTS in the foot. These practitioners claim to be CHANNELLING energy, and also removing blockages to energy currents through the body. They also claim to impart COSMIC ENERGY through the laying on of hands. The best a patient can expect is a pleasant foot or hand massage. This is a spiritual/psychic healing and is medically useless. Other similar techniques include Functional Integration or the Feldenkrais Method, the Alexander method, Rolfing, Do' In, Shiatsu, and Polarity Therapy.

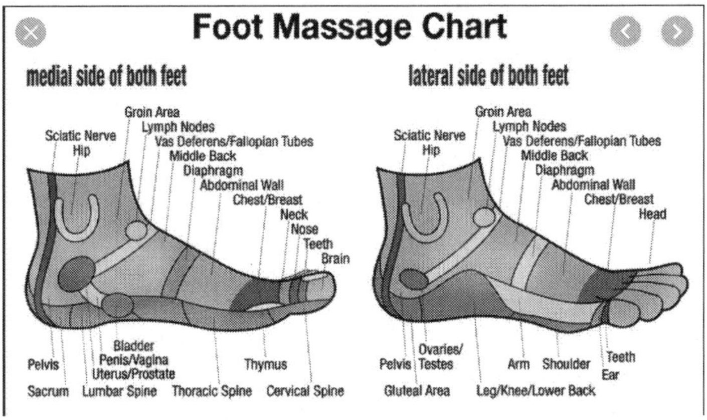

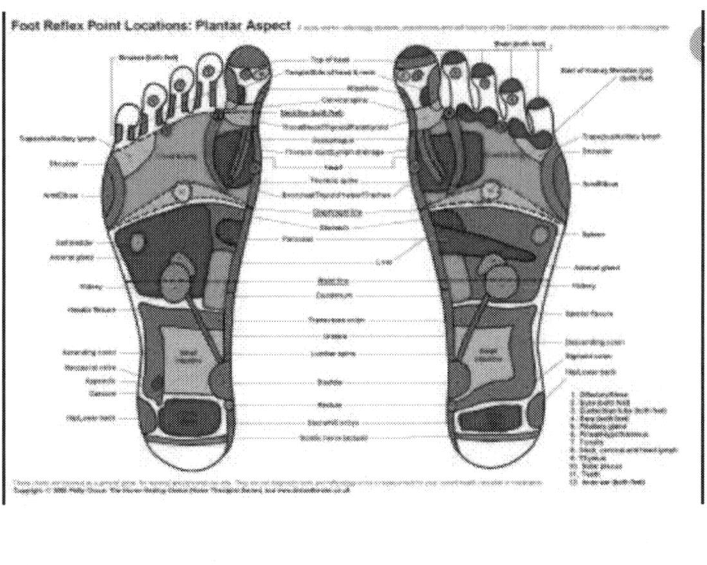

The charts claim to show which part of a human body may be healed if massaged. Some sell Reflexology insoles for your shoes for a similar effect. The claim that 7,000 nerve endings link directly with various body organs is medically false and misleading. Reflexology has never been called "a modern science" by medical scientists.

Reiki

This is one of the better known methods of occultic healing touch. It was developed by Mikao Usui, from Japan, who pretended to be a Christian. It is claimed that through the 'laying on of hands' a higher frequency of powerful cosmic healing energy can be tapped into. A person's psychic centres, or Chakras, are claimed to be injected with energy so their "Life Force" can be activated. Practitioners are initiated by a Reiki Master and there is a transmission of occult power. It should be pointed out very clearly this has nothing in common with the Biblical 'laying on of hands' for healing (see James 5:14-15), or appointment to an office as practiced in many Christian churches. Reiki is simply another term used to cover channelling demons into people, and should be avoided. This is probably one of the quicker ways to demonize someone. We cannot recommend this practice because of the occult basis and channeling "energy" or spirits into people. *(Recommended reading - "The Reiki Danger - Healing that Harms" by ES Harz, available from Jubilee Resources.)*

Rogerian Therapy

This is also known as ***"Person-Centred Psychotherapy."*** The therapist prompts (but tries not to direct) the patient towards a positive mental attitude, regardless of the source of any negative feelings or emotions, within or outside themselves. This therapy was named after its inventor, Carl Rogers (1902-1987).

Rolfing

Also known as ***"Structural Integration,"*** Rolfing was developed by Dr. Ida Rolf to assist better body posture, and to balance the "energy field" of the body, claiming that our human potential is expanded. This method involves lengthy manipulation and massage.

Shamanism

This is another term for a spirit-medium or a tribal witchdoctor. Shamanistic "medicine" utilizes incantations, plus herbal treatments and ritual dance to coax the spirits to bring healing to the patient. Most often the Shaman or witchdoctor would go into a trance, and would then be taken over by the spirit or demon during the healing session. Anyone receiving treatment from a Shaman is risking spirit possession and insanity (see Deuteronomy 18:10-13). Modern Shamans often advertise their services claiming "ancient knowledge" from native American Indians, New Zealand Maori, Hawaiian, Tibetan or South American cultures.

Shiatsu.

Originally based on Chinese acupuncture and acupressure, this is a Japanese art which uses the same acu-points on the same meridians to balance "Ki," the Japanese version of Ch'i. Because it is based on TCM/ Taoism and has an occultic/psychic basis, we cannot recommend it.

Silva Mind Control

This method was developed during the 1960's by American, Jose Silva, a man who "graduated" from Scientology. Silva's Mind Control utilizes auto suggestion and allegedly focuses on "integrating body and mind" so the mind can control physical matter through psychic power (see Revelation 18:23).

Tai Ch'i

A slow-motion version of martial arts where one movement begins as the end of the previous. It is claimed to activate the flow of Ch'i or Qi along meridian channels which have already been disproved. Moderate exercise is always helpful, especially as we grow older. This is a Taoist spiritual exercise as much as a physical exercise. We cannot recommend its use. (See Martial Arts, & See "Insights into Martial Arts, Tai Ch'i, TM & Yoga" on **back page**.)

Tarot Cards

These are a set of twenty two special cards which have various symbols printed on them. There are four main suits called Wands, Cups, Pentacles and Swords. One card has a skeleton claimed to represent an impending death. This is one of today's more popular methods of divination and contact with the spirit realm (see Zechariah 10:2).

Therapeutic Touch or Healing Touch

This method is used by many Alternative Practitioners these days and is even taught in some orthodox nursing schools. It is a good example of the ancient energy concept of ***"Prana"*** dressed for acceptability today (see sections on Energy and Chiropractic). This was developed by Dolores Krieger and Dora Kunz, both of whom were psychics - Kunz also being a leading Theosophist. Therapeutic Touch requires an Altered State of Consciousness to work best, and encourages the psychic abilities of the nurse/practitioner. Prana is the Hindu version of Universal Energy, where practitioners claim to CHANNEL this vital energy flow for the wellbeing of the sick. *"So a mystical concept is extracted from a distant corner of eastern philosophy, sanitized in western scientific trappings and then taught to well-intentioned members of the helping professions who are looking for new ways to relieve suffering,"* according to Wilson and Weldon. [30] Again it is simply a cover for channeling demons into people, and operating in the occult realm. There is a serious danger of misdiagnosis, and we cannot recommend it.

Traditional Chinese Medicine.

This involves diagnosis and treatment aimed at balancing the yin and yang in our bodies, (see page 31 for details). Treatments may include acupuncture, acupressure, Chinese herbal medicine, traditional Chinese massage, and moxibustion (the burning of a substance either on the skin or on an acupuncture needle). Even mental illness is seen as merely an imbalance of energy in the body. TCM is claimed to heal most conditions, but considering the occultic/psychic basis to these treatments we recommend avoidance.

Transcendental Meditation

This is taught as a non-religious meditation, and in some places it is being presented as an acceptable branch of medicine. The truth is that it is straight Hindu religious worship. The English translation of its Initiatory Puja or ritual prayer clearly states that the person is bowing down to fourteen different Hindu deities, and the teacher Guru Dev is bowed down to as deity (seventeen times in the second part). This Puja is simply a hymn of worship in Sanskrit.

Why are people refused an English language copy of what they are saying prior to or during their initiation? We wonder how many people have been tricked into this idolatry? Any Christian practicing T.M. is jeopardising their salvation, and should repent and cease involvement immediately. Many have come out from T.M. and having shed the consequences of idolatry have stated that T.M.'s claims are largely illusory, its results are mostly unhealthy and it is deceptive at every level.

Maharishi stated that T.M.'s goal is to permanently alter the meditator's perception of the world until it harmonizes with the Hindu pantheistic world view. The United States Federal Court legally identified T.M. as a religion (rather than a science) in 1976, which was upheld by the Court of Appeal in 1979. *"The entire mission of T.M. is to counter the ever spreading demon of Christianity,"* according to a senior spokesperson for T.M. in India in 1981. *(See "Insights into Martial Arts, Tai Ch'i, TM & Yoga" on back pages for more details.)*

Transpersonal Psychology or Psychosynthesis

This is a mixture of humanistic and analytical psychotherapeutic methods used for relationship and/or spiritual development. It was designed by Dr. Roberto Assagioli (1888-1974). This therapy is an attempt to harmonize a Western personality with the Eastern emphasis on higher levels of consciousness. Dreams, daydreams and various symbolic imagery are explored and speculated on.

Visualization/Guided Imagery

Developed by occultist, Mike Samuels, this practice attempts to conjure up in a person's minds a particular, perhaps painful, episode from the past, allegedly to help us come to terms with it. God is well able to bring to a person a vision or restore memory if He chooses. But the use of suggestion by a counselor talking their way through some imagined scene is not a Christian option. This is attempting to use Jesus as a ***"Spirit Guide."*** Manipulating a hurting person's imagination is cruel and dishonest because it pretends or fantasizes an unreal event. Christian counsellors should prayerfully point us to God who does meet the needs of the emotionally hurt. It is also important to use our wills to forgive. Roy Livesey said *"Believers in Jesus Christ walk in faith. Believing is not the same as imagining or visualising which are neither taught nor encouraged anywhere in Scripture. However visualizing is well understood by those familiar with the occult realm."* [31]

Great care should be taken to ensure it doesn't evolve into human potential or self-discovery exercises which are occult-related therapies. What is needed is compassion, the release of all bitterness and unforgiveness, and the understanding that Jesus Christ knows, loves and accepts the person regardless of their problems. Because of the contact with the spiritual realm while using this practice, we cannot recommend it.

Yoga

The word Yoga comes from the Sanskrit 'Yo' and 'ga' - Man and God/spirit, and the aim is to bring union between them. Like T.M. it is based firmly in Hinduism and every aspect has a spiritual purpose, despite claims to the contrary. Its basic belief is that the spiritual body is held in bondage to the physical body, and the Yogic posturing is supposed to manipulate the skeletal and muscular structure in order to release the spiritual body for union with the God-force. Yoga practice comes from sun and Baal worship which originated with Nimrod in Babylon, prior to its adoption by the early Hindus. Yoga has now developed into a form of spiritual worship to many Hindu deities, particularly Brahma, Vishnu and Shiva.

"There is no Yoga without Hinduism, it is the highest form - the very heart of it. The hope of immortality is Yoga," says an advanced Yoga instructor. The exercises are designed to move the SERPENT FORCE of ***Kundalini*** (the name of the demon) up the spine to the brain," and manifest in the so-called "third eye" in the centre of the forehead. The Bhagavadgita says Yoga is the way out of the reincarnation cycle. One method claimed to be 8,000 years old and from Tibet is called ***"The Radiance Technique"*** (or TRT). T.M, yoga and martial arts are not simply exercises; there is a spiritual bondage involved. If you need exercise then do it. Your doctor, gym or on line can surely give you some suggestions which don't involve worshipping Hindu demon-gods. We cannot recommend Yoga. *(See "Insights into Martial Arts, Tai Ch'i, TM & Yoga" on back pages for more details.)*

Zen Therapy

This is firmly based in Buddhism, and claims to integrate the person holistically, body, soul and spirit, using meditation.

Zone Therapies

There are several of these, including some mentioned above. Acupuncture and reflexology are probably the best known of them. It is claimed that different sections of a person's body part (e.g. a foot, ear, hand, etc.) are a microcosm of the whole person, and so pressing or massaging a particular spot will bring healing to the relevant body organ. (See acupuncture.) There is no medical or scientific basis to zone therapies, and any healing claimed would possibly have happened anyway due to the body's repair mechanism. Other possibilities include psychosomatic and/or hypnotic trances inducing a spiritualist healing.

Other Forms of Divination

Let us remember that Divination is *"obtaining knowledge by forbidden magical means."* ***Clairvoyance*** is an inner or mental picture, given by demonic power, which usually relates to health or personal problems. This is frequently practiced in Spiritualist Churches to aid their 'healing' diagnosis. It is a form of witchcraft, and a counterfeit of the Biblical "Word of Knowledge," (1 Corinthians 12:8). ***Numerology*** studies the occult significance of numbers. Seances attempt to contact the dead, often as a 'fun game' but in truth they are contacting demonic spirits who knew the dead person while they were alive. It is impossible to consult the dead, as they are either in heaven or hell. God tells us in the Bible there is no possibility of such communication (e.g. Luke 16:22-25).

The authors cannot recommend any of the above therapies or practices. The danger of occult bondages which are virtually certain to occur to any patient, and which seem to affect most if not all these therapists. There are safer and better ways to health and healing which we now wish to propose to the reader. But first, let us summarize the things to beware of.

Let The Patient Beware!

When people ask what they should avoid, for their own and their family's protection, we suggest the following principles we have gleaned from a variety of sources. [32]

BEWARE of therapies which are "energy-based," where invisible energies are claimed to be manipulated or which rely on psychic anatomies. Examples include acupuncture, acutouch, muscle-testing, reflexology, and color therapy.

BEWARE of therapists who utilize psychic knowledge, powers or abilities. Examples include clairvoyant diagnosis, psychic healing or surgery, crystal healing, therapeutic touch, radionics and psychometry, channeling energies and shamanistic medicine.

BEWARE of therapies which virtually no-one has heard of. Examples we have heard of are Terpsichoretrancetherapy, or TTT; and Esogetic Colorpuncture.

BEWARE of any therapy which has yet to be validated by science. Virtually all New Age medicine is either quackery, occult power, or its value or safety remains undemonstrated.

BEWARE of therapists who claim they can cure just about everything. Such therapies, far from curing almost everything, usually cure almost nothing. Examples include color therapy, acupuncture, homoeopathy, and some chiropractic.

BEWARE of bizarre or senseless explanations. A homeopath will claim that their strongest medicine is the most diluted, a color therapist may ask you to drink water bathed in "yellow rays" to help cure your indigestion, or astrological medicine practitioner may tell you that Jupiter is affecting your nucleic acids.

BEWARE of therapies for which the primary proof is the testimonies of satisfied clients. Virtually all new age medicine is in this realm but that doesn't validate any method or practice.

BEWARE of therapies which rely on altered states of consciousness. These are notoriously deceptive, unreliable in health matters and frequently open the doors to spiritualist influences. Examples include hypnotic regression, and many types of meditation and visualization techniques.

BEWARE of those whose sincerity is intended to cover up their lack of medical or scientific legitimacy.

BEWARE of techniques which have been scientifically disproved. Examples include iridology, homeopathy, astrological medicine, radionics, and some aspects of chiropractic.

BEWARE of therapists who claim to be able to diagnose or treat patients on the basis of intuition. This is usually only spirit divination by another term.

BEWARE of any therapist who claims their methods are specially connected to God. Their "divine" intuition probably comes from a spirit which doesn't have your best interests at heart, despite any apparent healing.

BEWARE of any therapist who has not graduated from a recognized or accredited medical school. Some medical doctors are "closet psychics," in which case some of the above points will guide you.

BEWARE of retailers who sell questionable products and therapies. What they are promoting may endanger the physical, emotional or spiritual health of customers. Making a lot of money is not a good enough reason to sell something. While there are legal steps which may be taken against those who provide wrong advice, there is a higher judge who will ultimately hold each of us accountable for our actions.

BEWARE of unsolicited advice from "friends," practitioners or therapists who tell you there is something wrong with you - something of which you have no symptoms and are completely unaware of. Use your common sense!

Suggestions prior to involvement in any alternative therapy.

1. On no account get involved purely on the advice of a well-meaning friend.

2. Search out as much as possible about the history and proven facts of the therapy, and also the beliefs of it's founder.

3. Ascertain the mode of manufacture, and the claims made for its working.

4. Most importantly, ascertain what are the spiritual, moral and ethical fruits shown in the lives of both the practitioners and known consumers, their spouses and children.

Foods which are Good for us, and Why [37]

Sources used below here include: www.nutriwatch.org; wwwquackwatch.com; US National Institutes of Health Clinical Center - www.cc.nih.gov.; Psychologist Ellen Coleman - www.hcrc.org; Charles Sturt University, NSW Australia - www.csu.edu.au; www.safetyalerts.com; US Federal Dept. of Agriculture; University of California Berkeley - www.berkeleywellness.com.

Oats: Soluble fibre b-glucan. Reduces cholesterol, heart disease & stroke.

Soy: Proteins. Reduces cholesterol. Cancer risk. (Apparently 98% of world's soy has been genetically modified, making it suspect for that reason alone.)

Flaxseed Oil: Essential fatty acids including omega-3 & lignans. Reduces cholesterol.

Nuts: (including peanuts). Mono & polyunsaturated fats, folate, vitamins, minerals, anti-oxidants. Many benefits of other listed foods.

Tomatoes: Lycoprene (a carotenoid). Reduces risk of cancer, in particular prostate cancer.

Garlic/Onions: Allium chemicals. May reduce risk of cancer when eaten raw.

Broccoli family: (includes cauliflower, cabbage, brussel sprouts): Reduced risk of cancer, in particular, breast cancer.

Citrus fruits: Folates, vitamin C, fibre. Reduces cancer risk.

Cranberry/Blueberry: Fructose and a polymeric compound. Treats urinary Tract infections, antimicrobial.

Grapes/wine: Flavonoids in grape skins. Like other anti-oxidants, decreases risk of heart disease & stroke. However, wine drinking can increase cancer risk.

Fish: Omega-3 fatty acids. Probably reduces risk of heart disease & stroke.

Dairy Products: Calcium. Good for bones, may reduce colon cancer.

Beef: Conjugated linoleic acid. Reduces cancer risk.

The Good, the Bad and the Dangerous

Tiptoeing through the Alternative/complementary health care products minefield. Please note well - "Natural" doesn't always mean "safe!"

CODE: ✔ = Proven Benefits

? = Inconclusive, or not all claims proven.

✖ = Not proven or inconclusive.

Aloe Vera

? Indoor plant. Multipurpose folk remedy. Proven laxative. Inconclusive tests on claimed benefits for skin, ulcers, diabetes, cancer, headaches, arthritis, immune system deficiencies.

Anti-Oxidants

? Vitamin C, Vitamin E, bete-carotene (which the body converts into vitamin A) found in fruits & vegetables. May slow down aging process & reduce risk of age-related diseases such as heart disease and stroke. However, anti-oxidants in food may be more effective than eating them as isolated chemicals in supplements.

Arnica

✔ Daisy-like flower. Contains known anti-inflammatory & pain-relieving chemicals. Promotes white blood cells to treat bruised tissue. May help treat arthritis, eczema, burns, boils, acne. Poisonous when eaten.

Aromatherapy

✖ Pleasant fragrances obtained by plants to influence body function such as relaxation, & removing toxins. No scientific evidence of benefits.

Bach Flower Remedies

? British doctor Edward Bach developed 38 remedies based on flower essences to treat a wide range of emotional states. Disputed. (Remedies based on divination.)

Bee Products (Pollen, Royal Jelly, Propolis)

? Bees take pollen from plants to hives. Royal Jelly is fed to newly-hatched grubs and queen bees. Plants make propolis to protect emerging buds, which bees use to disinfect hives. Pollen and Royal Jelly are supposed to boost energy, which sceptics say are no different from ordinary foods. Propolis has proven anti-microbial properties and is used to soothe sore throats.

Calcium Gluconate

✔ Supplement. Prevent or reduce onset or progress of Osteoporosis (brittle bones, particularly in aging women).

Comfrey

✔ Leafy herb. As a poultice treats warts, eczema & other skin problems. Poisonous if eaten.

Dietary Supplements (see vitamins & Minerals)

✔ Useful for people who are unable or unwilling to eat a balanced diet.

Echinacea

? Herb, member of daisy family. Native American traditional medicine. May prevent onset of colds & 'flu. Studies inconclusive.

Evening Primrose Oil

? Extract from Native American wildflower, not a true primrose. Supposed to help treat skin diseases, reduce cholesterol, & other conditions. Studies inconclusive.

Folic Acid

✔ Important for pregnant women. Can be taken as a supplement or in folate-rich foods, such as leafy greens, some cereals, beans, peas other vegetables.

Ginger

? Root herb popular in Asian cuisine & herbal medicines. May help treat nausea, hypoglycaemia (lack of blood sugar), & act as an anti-inflammatory. More testing needed to prove health claims.

Ginko

? Many purported benefits. The main ones, improving memory & treating dementia, have been disproven.

Ginseng

? Root of Asian herb. Supposed to boost mental health, physical & sexual stamina & promote longevity. Evidence of benefits contradictory, may cause unpleasant side-effects such as nosebleeds, high blood pressure.

Homeopathy

✖ Extremely diluted preparations of an active ingredient are supposed to retain the spirit of the essence of that substance, even if none of the ingredient is present in the final product. No scientific evidence of benefits. (Disproven by Australian Federal Govt. Scientific Report.)

Iron

✔ For healthy red blood cells. Taken as supplement, or particularly in meat, fish & poultry.

Magnesium

✔ Every cell needs it. Taken as supplement, or particularly in spinach, nuts, seeds, whole grains. This does aid sleep.

Placebo Effect

✔ If you believe a treatment will work, the chances of it working are increased.

Saw Palmetto

✝ Helps reduce symptoms of enlarged prostate gland in men. Evidence lacking on whether this plant prevent long-term prostate problems.

Selenium

✔ Essential anti-oxidant chemical. Taken as supplement, or in seafood, meat, nuts. Some soils are naturally-selenium poor, compensated for by the addition of selenium to fertilizer, animal feed and bread production.

Sports Supplements

✔ People who burn an extremely high amount of calories may boost food intake with supplements. Alternatively, try eating healthy food such as fruit, vegetables and meat.

St. John's Wort

? Herb. Proven mild anti-depressant. However, pregnant women should avoid it. May interact with other medicines & become toxic.

Valerian

? Herbal remedy. Supposed sedative & stress reliever. May cause upset stomach, raised heart beat, headaches. Non-addictive.

Vitamin A

✔ For vision & bone growth. Taken as a supplement or in fortified breakfast cereals, & dark-colored fruits & vegetables.

Vitamin B6

✔ For most body processes. Taken as a supplement or in fortified breakfast cereals, beans, red meat, poultry, fish, some fruits & vegetables.

Vitamin 12

✔ For healthy nerve & red blood cells. Taken as a supplement, or in fortified breakfast cereals, fish, dairy products, eggs, red meat, poultry.

Vitamin B15

✖ Supposed to have nutritional properties. Not proven.

Vitamin C

? Supposed to prevent & treat cold & 'flu. Inconclusive.

Vitamin D

✔ Maintains normal levels of calcium & phosphorus, important for bones. Made in the body after exposure to sunlight, or eaten in fatty fish, such as salmon or cod liver oil.

Vitamin E

✔ Anti-oxidant (see separate heading). Taken as a supplement, or in vegetable oils, nuts & green leafy vegetables.

Zinc

✔ Essential trace element, taken as a supplement, or in seafood, red meat, poultry, beans, nuts, fortified breakfast cereals, whole grains, dairy products. May prevent some prostate problems.

Essential Safety Tips About Herbs

* **Consult your physician before using herbs.** This is particularly important if you have a chronic condition - such as hypertension or diabetes - or take any other medicines. Some herbs interact with drugs, especially blood thinners, sedatives and antidepressants.

* **Follow Label Directions.** Different brands of herbal supplements vary in strength. Always take the manufacturer's recommended dosage, unless your doctor tells you otherwise.

* **Start with a Low Dose.** Herbal dosages are often given as a range - for example, '400 to 600 milligrams three times a day.' If you don't get sufficient relief from the lowest dose, gradually increase it. (Don't take more than the maximum amount.) If there is still no benefit, see your physician.

* **Pay Attention to Your Body.** Sensitive people may have adverse effects even at low doses. If any unusual symptoms occur within eight hours of taking a herbal remedy, stop using it.

* **Pregnant?** Don't try herbs. Also, you shouldn't give herbs to children under the age of two.

God's Plan For Health And Healing

In practical terms, most people (wisely) get medical help. Since the cause of most sickness (and its attendant misery) is of a spiritual nature, the best cure for organic and mental disease is spiritual. The disobedience of Adam and Eve brought sin into the world, and with sin, death came upon them and all succeeding generations, (Romans 5:12). The day our first parents rebelled against God was the day they began to die, spiritually, physically, emotionally and mentally.

The sins of parents often result in the sickness of their children. We have read of children being born drunk or drugged because the mother had taken alcohol or drugs prior to the birth. Foetal alcohol syndrome can also cause deformities of the baby and mental retardation. Also a child may be born blind because the parents have a venereal disease. Nevertheless, as Jesus said many times, the sickness is not always the result of sin in either the afflicted person or their parents, (see John 9:3); the cause may be even still further back. Obviously if Adam and Eve hadn't sinned, there wouldn't be sickness in the world.

Our bodies are so made by God that normally they resist disease. For example, there are strong bacteria in our throats and there are cells in our bodies that have the potential to develop into cancer, but these are kept in check by our God-given immune system. These only become a problem when our immunity level drops, and this has no bearing on "Energy." If this were not so the human race would soon be destroyed. But if for any reason the natural defences of the body are weakened, disease has a good opportunity to secure a foothold. Undue physical strain, failure to take care of the body properly, or just plain sin may weaken its natural resistance. However, it all comes back to obedience to God. Read the 28th chapter of Deuteronomy. The first 14 verses list the many blessings God promised to bestow on the obedient, and the last 54 verses list the many curses of God on the disobedient and rebellious. The question may arise as to where disease itself came from. The answer the Bible gives is that Satan, the evil one, is the author of disease. The story of Job tells us that God built an invisible hedge around him so the devil couldn't touch him. But for reasons space won't permit here, one day God withdrew His protection, and permitted Satan to afflict Job with painful boils. Notice that although God gave the permission, it was actually Satan who inflicted the boils on Job, (Job 2:7). Later God answered Job's cry and healed him completely.

There is also the case of the woman with the infirmity whom Jesus healed. This woman had been oppressed for eighteen years with a spirit of infirmity. Jesus revealed the cause of her sickness in His conversation with the religious rulers, that it was Satan who had bound the woman. **"Then should not this woman, a daughter of Abraham, whom Satan has kept bound for eighteen long years, be set free on the Sabbath day from what bound her?"** (Luke 13:16). Note also when Peter was speaking of Christ, he connected the ministry of healing with deliverance from Satanic oppression; **"How God anointed Jesus of Nazareth with the Holy Spirit and with power; who went about doing good, and healing all that were oppressed of the devil; for God was with him,"** (Acts 10:38).

Thus we see that healing was in effect liberating people from the oppression of Satan. Nor is this just poetic language. As we witness and study the miracles of Jesus Christ, we often find that evil spirits were involved in the cause of the sickness. These had to be cast out before the person could be made well. The Bible speaks of deaf spirits, dumb spirits, insane spirits, infirm spirits, deceiving spirits, seducing spirits, lying spirits, familiar spirits, spirits of divination, perverse spirits, wicked spirits, unclean spirits, and foul spirits, and let's not forget Legion! All these have different ways of afflicting or deceiving people. Satan's power over people varies with the individual. In many cases he merely oppresses them. Many Christians are oppressed by the enemy simply because they have not learned to take their authority in Christ and rebuke him. The devil cannot actually possess a true Christian, but he can oppress him or her. Believers must learn to take authority over the oppressor in the name and authority of Jesus Christ.

On the other hand there are, unfortunately, more people than we would like to believe who are actually demon-possessed. Some become completely controlled by Satan, which is a major cause of insanity. Rev. David Pawson (from the UK) quoted some statistics which revealed that some 24% of British psychiatric patients had been deeply involved in Spiritualism. Such persons have no power of their own to exercise faith for deliverance. They are like the demon-possessed man whom Jesus met in the tombs (Mark 5:1-19); unless someone exercises faith for them, they may never recover. Almost one-quarter of the New Testament verses about the ministry of Jesus involve evicting evil spirits. That is not insignificant. Some might want deliverance from the sickness, but not from their sins. We must remember that the promise is a twofold cure from a twofold curse. **"Bless the Lord, oh my soul, and forget not all his benefits. He forgives all my sins, and heals all my diseases,"** (Psalm 103:2-3). The promise calls for deliverance from sin first then deliverance from sickness.

When Hezekiah, King of Israel, was sick to the point of death, he turned his face to the wall and prayed. God heard his prayer and said, **"I have heard your prayer and seen your tears; I will heal you. On the third day from now you will go up to the temple of the Lord,"** (2 Kings 20:5). Some people in seeking healing have little thought of serving the Lord afterwards, but not Hezekiah. On the third day he went up to the Temple of the Lord, and worshipped God, thanking Him for his great deliverance.

Jesus healed a crippled man who lay for 38 years in an absolutely helpless condition at the pool of Bethesda. Afterwards, the Lord said to him, **"See, you are well again. Stop sinning or something worse may happen to you,"** (John 5:14). Certainly Jesus made it plain that continuation in sin might lead to a worse condition, (see Luke 11:24-26). Here is a hint that this man's affliction was possibly caused by previous sin in his life. *(This and related issues are covered in much greater details in "Biblical Healing Training Manual" shown on the back pages.)*

Divine Health

Every Christian should grasp one of the most important truths about healing. Even though it is God's will to heal us when we are sick, His perfect plan is not for us to be continually in need of more healing, but to live in Divine Health and strength as revealed in 3 John 2. **"Beloved, I wish above all things that you may prosper and be in health, even as your soul prospers."** He will renew our strength as an eagle (Psalm 103:5). We believe Divine Health means the restoration of the body's system in all ways so the person has no further need of medication, etc. Continuing medication is not Divine Health. Just as it is not God's will that we be saved over and over again, but that we remain spiritually well, it is not really God's best that He heal us over and over again, but that we ***"Be in health."*** Thus, whenever Satan tries to put any illness or infirmity onto our bodies, we should immediately take these same steps to force him to withdraw before he gets a stronghold on our physical being the same way we would rebuff an attack on our spiritual being.

When God gave the covenant of healing to the children of Israel, He did not emphasize healing so much as He did Divine Health. He said that if Israel was obedient to the commandments of the Lord, disease and sickness, which had come on the Egyptians, would not come on the Israelites, (Exodus 15:26). In case the people of Israel should misunderstand the real meaning of the covenant of healing, the Lord repeated the promise in slightly different words in Exodus 23:25 & 26, **"Worship the Lord your God, and His blessing will be on your food and water. I will take away sickness from among you, and none will miscarry or be barren in your land. I will give you a full life span."** The promise is repeated, and the condition is repeated. In the book of Deuteronomy, the promise of Divine Health and immunity from sickness is repeated yet again; "The Lord will keep you free from every disease. He will not inflict on you the horrible diseases you knew in Egypt, but He will inflict them on all who hate you," (Deuteronomy 7:15).

It is interesting to note that the book of Deuteronomy concludes with the observation that if the plagues and sicknesses of Egypt should appear among the people of God, it would be a sign of their disobedience, (Deuteronomy 28:15-28.) The remarkable thing is that the children of Israel did for a considerable period appropriate and live under the blessings of the promise. There were exceptions when some of the people disobeyed God. There were jealousies, murmuring, and lusts that resulted in bringing plagues upon themselves. But as a whole while they wandered in the wilderness the people were immune to sickness. As a result, the Psalmist could say **"He brought out Israel, laden with silver and gold, and from among their tribes, no-one faltered."** (Psalm 105:37). The Scripture gives us examples of those who enjoyed divine health.

One was Moses who had reached the advanced age of one hundred and twenty-years. In the natural, we might suppose he had reached extreme senility and feebleness, yet he retained the virility of youth until the day he died, (Deuteronomy 34:7). Caleb was much the same, and in Joshua 14:10 &11 it mentions how he went out to war at the age of 85. He used a sword, not a walking stick.

It is evident that one reason we have so much sickness in the church today is that we have restricted, neglected or ignored God's promises. Some have restricted the Promises to the Old Testament. Others are ignorant of the promises altogether because they don't know the Bible. But if we obey God's commands, and live in right fellowship with Him, then it is our absolute right to His promise for Divine Health. Thus, when Satan attempts, (as he may do) to put sickness or disease on our bodies, we should not wait until we are overcome with sickness. At the first sign of attack from Satan, we must rise up and rebuke him. **"Resist the devil, and he will flee from you,"** (James 4:7). However, we must not overlook the first part of this verse, which states **"Submit yourselves to God..."** We can only drive Satan off when we are submitted to God and have the Holy Spirit guiding us in the battle. The Bible teaches that it is God's will that the believer should have a long and useful life, blessed with health and strength. One of the better medicines is the 91st Psalm which should be meditated on.

Of course every promise has a condition. The condition is that the individual will be satisfied with the good things of heaven, and not preoccupy him or herself with an unhealthy preoccupation with the things of this earth. We must soar like an eagle above the petty things of this world. We must learn to dwell in the heavenly places with Christ Jesus, (Ephesians 2:6). We would direct the reader's attention to the words of Proverbs, which inform us that if we diligently give heed to the word of God, then we can claim the promise of Divine Health. **"My Son, pay attention to what I say; listen closely to my words. Do not let them out of your sight, keep them within your heart; for they are life to those who find them and health to a man's whole body,"** (Proverbs 4:20-22). We should point out that anyone involved in an effective Christian ministry will suffer many more spiritual attacks than most people, including on their health. Discouragement, relationship difficulties, and character assassinations are also popular tools of the enemy of our souls. Although such matters often affect us in the physical realm, there is no doubt it is a spiritual battle.

While the children of Israel wandered in the wilderness for 40 years, and while God waited for a generation to die out (because of their disobedience and grumbling) God gave the Ten Commandments on Mt. Sinai, and through Moses He also gave many instructions to the people. God wanted them to live holy lives, to be a nation of priests who would worship only Him. What was His first Commandment? **"You shall have no other Gods before me."** God needed to say that, because in Egypt the people worshipped the sun, cats, snakes, lions and many other false deities. God doesn't want us to worship anything else, not money, or power, or anything we own or want to, only God. What was the second commandment? Briefly, **"You shall not make any idols or bow and worship them."** You see, God is a jealous God; He won't share His glory with anyone, let alone some trivial object of stone, wood or gold. We are not to worship things that men have created, but the Master Creator Himself.

Prior to letting the Israelites occupy the Promised Land, God instructed them to totally destroy every living thing in Canaan. That sounds very harsh but God had good reason, for the inhabitants of that land were involved in the most despicable forms of idolatry and sin. They worshipped a variety of gods, but the main three were Baal, Asherah and Molech. These stood for material prosperity, uninhibited sexual expression, and child sacrifice. Sounds familiar to today's problems with materialism, immorality and abortion, doesn't it. Now you understand why God wanted His people to cleanse Canaan. They failed to do so properly, and were later snared by this idolatry themselves. Here's what God told them to do. "When you enter the land the Lord your God is giving you, do not learn to imitate the detestable ways of the nations there. Let no one be found among you who sacrifices his son or daughter in the fire, who practices divination or sorcery, interprets omens, engages in witchcraft, or casts spells, or who is a medium or spiritist, or who consults the dead. Anyone who does these things is detestable to the Lord, and because of these detestable practise the Lord your God will drive out those nations before you. You must be blameless before the Lord your God. The nations you will dispossess listen to those who practice sorcery or divination. but as for you, the Lord your God has not permitted you to do so," (Deuteronomy 18:9-14). Space prevents us from a deep discussion on these points, but we will list many of Satan's snares for the people of today at the end of this book.

Does God Want To Heal You?

Only the Scriptures can provide the true answer to the question, "Does God want to heal you?" We believe that God answers clearly through His word, so no-one should misunderstand it. A leper came to Jesus not knowing for certain whether it was His will to cleanse him of his leprosy. In his ignorance he said, **"Lord, if you are willing, you can make me clean."** At once Jesus proved for all time that it is His will by reaching out His hand and touching the poor leper, saying, **"I am willing; be clean,"** (Matthew 8:2-3). The Scriptures teach from the beginning that it is God's will to heal. No sooner had God redeemed His people from Egypt than He gave them the covenant of healing. He actually made it a law, (Exodus 15:25). He went further and told them that if they obey His statutes and commandments, they wouldn't get sick; **"If you listen carefully to the voice of the Lord your God and do what is right in His eyes, if you pay attention to His commands and keep all His decrees, I will not bring on you any of the diseases I brought on the Egyptians, for I am the Lord who heals you,"** (Exodus 15:26).

Another promise to those who put their trust in God comes from Psalm 91:10. **"Then no harm will befall you, no disaster will come near your tent."** Centuries later when Jesus began His ministry, He preached one of His first sermons in His home city of Nazareth, and this was the text He used; **"The Spirit of the Lord is on me, because he has anointed me to preach good news to the poor. He has sent me to proclaim freedom for the prisoners and recovery of sight for the blind, to release the oppressed, to proclaim the year of the Lord's favor,"** (Luke 4:18-19).

Jesus not only healed the sick, but committed that same ministry to His disciples. **"Calling the Twelve to him, he sent them out two by two and gave them authority over evil spirits. They went out and preached that people should repent. They drove out many demons and anointed many sick people with oil and healed them,"** (Mark 6:7,12-13). And later when He gave them the Great Commission, He included the promise of healing to all believers in Mark 16:16-18.

"Whoever believes and is baptized will be saved, but whoever does not believe will be condemned. And these signs will accompany those who believe; in my name they will drive out demons; they will speak in new tongues; they will pick up snakes with their hands; and when they drink deadly poison, it will not hurt them at all; they will place their hands on sick people, and they will get well." The promise was not only for the Apostles, but is still valid today to all who believe in Jesus Christ. Nowhere in the Scriptures is there the slightest hint that God's command for praying for the sick has ever been revoked, but rather **"He is the same, Yesterday, Today and Forever,"** (John 14:6).

Just as God gave a promise of healing to the people in the wilderness, so God gave a command authorizing the ministry of healing in the church in the New Testament. **"Is any one of you sick? He should call the elders of the church to pray over him and anoint him with oil in the name of the Lord. And the prayer offered in faith will make the sick person well; the Lord will raise him up. If he has sinned, he will be forgiven. Therefore confess your sins to each other so that you may be healed. The prayer of a righteous man is powerful and effective,"** (James 5:14 - 16).

What about doctors and nurses? We would not want to reflect in any way against the vast majority of the medical profession. There are stories about doctors loading their patients with heaps of pills etc., until they become drug addicts, but these are comparatively minor in proportion. Generally, the medical profession has done a great work in alleviating the ills of humanity. After God gave Israel the covenant of healing, He also taught them health laws and appointed certain officials to administer those laws. The world needs specially trained men and women to teach people the proper care of their bodies. Jesus did not criticise those who cared for the sick and wounded, (Luke 10:34). He said that those who are sick have need of a physician, (Matthew 9:12). Mothers for example need special care at the time of the birth of their children. All thoughtful persons appreciate the value of help that trained personnel can give the sick. But doctors can only go so far; even they will confess they can only assist nature. In His graciousness God has given us the assurance of a well body if we accept His word. An assurance no less definite than the promise He has given us of health for our soul.

The Problem Of Failures In Healing

Why are some healed and others not? We have sought many opinions on this subject, realizing that at the end of it all, God is still sovereign. Some people seek physical or emotional healing without caring about the spiritual consequences. While understandable in some cases, this is a short-sighted view. To reveal something of the range of views on this, we show here three different lists. The authors know of many people who have gone through these lists, repented of sin, unforgiveness etc., done serious business with God, and been healed, sometimes in a miraculous way. Readers are invited to do the same.
Hindrances to Healing [33]

1. Disobedience towards God. (Exodus 20:1-6; 1 Samuel 15:23; John 3:3-7; Deuteronomy 5:16)

2. Lack of Knowledge about the Word of God. (Isaiah 5:13; Proverbs 4:20-23; Hosea 4:6; Psalm 34:15-18; Psalm 103:3-5; Isaiah 53:5; 1 Peter 2:24)

3. Lack of Faith. (Mark 11:24; John 11:4, 42-43; Hebrews 12:2; Hebrews 11:6; Romans 14:23)

4. Unbelief. (Mark 6:5-6; Hebrews 3:12-13)

5. Unconfessed Sin. (1 Corinthians 6:9-10; Galatians 5:19-21; Ephesians 5:4-6)

6. Unforgiveness. (Matthew 6:14-15; 18:34-35)

7. Rejection. (Ephesians 1:6) We are accepted by God - we need to accept ourselves.

8. Involvement in the Occult. (Exodus 20:3; & 23:24-26; Deuteronomy 18:9-13; Galatians 5:20)

9. Idolatrous Oaths, e.g. Freemasonry, Druids, Secret Societies, Nursing and many other medical oaths which honor Egyptian, Greek and Roman deities. (Exodus 20:7; Leviticus 5:4-5; Matthew 5:33-37; James 5:12; Isaiah 44:8)

10. Neglect of the Poor. (Matthew 25:31-41; Isaiah 58:6-8 &10-11; Psalm 41:3)

11. Curses. (Deuteronomy 28)

12. Unconfessed & Hidden Anger. (Ephesians 4:31-32; Colossians 3:8)

13. Lack of Peace of Mind. (Hebrews 4:9-11; John 14:27; John 20:21; Proverbs 16:3; Philippians 4:6-9)

14. Fear. (2 Timothy 1:7; 1 John 4:18)

15. Ungodly Soul Ties. Usually from wrong sexual or spiritual relationships, or domination by others. (1 Corinthians 6:16-20; 2 Corinthians 6:14-17)

16. Sickness caused by Demonic Activity. (Mark 1:34; 9:25-26; Psalm 118:17)

(I taught about the above in a Baptist Church in New Zealand, and led people through a brief prayer for each topic. As we did this, people were spontaneously healed by the Holy Spirit all over the auditorium. It seems God is more willing to heal than we are to put things right with Him.)

Francis MacNutt suggests eleven reasons for failure; [34]

1. Lack of faith.

2. Redemptive suffering.

3. False value attached to suffering.

4. Sin.

5. Failure to pray specifically.

6. Faulty diagnosis.

7. Refusal to see medicine as a means through which God heals.

8. Failure to use natural means to preserve health, e.g. taking exercise.

9. The time may not be right..

10. A different person is to be the instrument of healing.

11. The Social environment prevents healing from taking place.

Lawrence Althouse suggests six reasons for failure;

1. Sometimes the sick person, either consciously or unconsciously, chooses to hold onto their sickness.

2. The sick person may continue to surround themselves with those very same influences which led to their sickness.

3. Healing may be hindered when the sick one is surrounded by an atmosphere that is unreceptive or hostile to healing.

4. Healing prayer may be ineffective because we are too narrow in our praying, and refuse to let God be God to fulfil His will in and through us.

5. Sometimes we do not give God enough of ourselves with which to work.

6. We forget that healing of the body is not the only, or even the highest, goal in the healing ministry. The healing of the soul and spirit is more important.

Emily Gardner Neal says: *"No one who understands spiritual healing will ever turn away from God because he is not physically healed for no one who ever turns to God in faith remains spiritually unhealed. No one who has experienced a healing of the spirit would ever exchange what he has received for a purely physical cure."*

It is our observation that much sickness in Christians is avoidable and reversible if they will only put themselves right with God and other people. Some people demand a physical healing regardless of the spiritual costs, which is short-sighted and foolish. Regardless of anyone's beliefs God is sovereign. There are times when physical healing does not happen. If we can't trust God with our health and welfare, then our spiritual salvation will have little value. Trusting God in all things is the only Biblical answer.

Anyone who has been involved in any of the above alternative practices which are described earlier in this book, should repent (turn away from) and renounce it in the name of Jesus Christ. Then you need to follow the instructions God laid down in the Bible. (See James 5:14-16, mentioned earlier.)

What do we do next? We need to believe what the Lord says about us, and to get into the Word of God. There are a lot of Self cults operating now in many areas. "I can do it myself." Be content with what the Lord has given you, and do not become too obsessed about exercise, dieting etc. It is good to exercise and to control your diet, but watch out for the dieting cults (recent medical research shows that about 96% of diet regimes have no long-term improvement).

Watch out if you have to buy your food from only one particular person or shop; you don't know the sorts of prayers prayed over the items before they are displayed in the shop. Just take the old grandmother's advice, "a little bit of everything and you'll be alright." Live in moderation.

As a Christian take a break, have a rest, read your Bible and get into prayer. A lot of things which the Lord wants to heal or sort out in your life will be done if only we believers will get into prayer. If you are sick, read James 5:14-16, be prayed for, then go and see your medical doctor. If you are in any doubt about what your doctor is doing to you, ask and they will tell you. If they say they are taking care of your spiritual health, ask them which medical college trained them to take care of spiritual health? There is none. They are trained to take care of physical health. If they say, "Well, I am giving you these to control your mind," ask them where they learned mental healing, are they a psychiatrist? If they are not, then be very wary.

Above all, seek after God and His will for your life, and keep in fellowship with fellow believers. There are a lot of things around in the Alternative Health area which are dangerous. Don't be afraid to ask questions of your doctors, your pastors, etc.

(If the reader wishes to learn the concepts of Biblical healing, one of the authors has put together a comprehensive ***Biblical Healing Training Manual,*** and taught this on five continents, with many healed, but more importantly, teams of Christians now holding regular healing services as a major form of evangelism. Details on pages at end of this book.)

Hereditary Illnesses & Ancestral Curses

We need to reconcile the fact that God's blessings are conditional. When we obey, we enjoy. When we disobey, we incur curses. There appears to be no neutral ground. The same God who blesses also allows curses to come into our lives when we refuse to repent. It is not a coincidence that whenever blessings are pronounced in the Bible, there are curses pronounced nearby.

In Deuteronomy 28 there are 14 verses dealing with blessings and 54 verses which deal with curses. Deuteronomy 27 deals mainly with curses. The emphasis appears to be more on curses than blessings. The Lord does not want us to be curse hunters - seeing curses under every table. We need to concentrate on the positive aspects of God's Word. But God's promise of blessing, no matter how often it is pronounced on a person, will not be fulfilled if there is a curse operating in that person's life. A curse seems to function as a demon directed or permitted to afflict a person. Curses then seem to act as shields or fences around demonic spirits, preventing their eviction until the curse is broken. We may have brought it on ourselves, or inherited it, or through the use of sorcery or other types of witchcraft the curse may have been sent to trouble us.

In Joshua 7 Israel could not take little Ai because the whole nation of Israel came under a curse because of one person, Achan. Many Christians are unable to be victorious in their Christian lives because among other causes, curses may be operating in their lives. It is important first to break the curse so the person can enjoy his or her blessings. The affliction may take several forms. The following list is complied by Dr. Derek Prince based on Deuteronomy 28. [35]

1. Mental and emotional disorders.
2. Repeated or chronic sickness (often hereditary).
3. Barrenness, miscarriage and female reproductive problems.
4. Breakdowns of marriage and family alienation.

5. Continuing financial insufficiency (regardless of income level).

6. Being "accident-prone."

7. History of suicides and unnatural or untimely deaths.

Any one on its own may not involve a curse, although it may. Several of these obvious in a family would almost certainly indicate a curse in action. Dr. Prince mentions the Kennedy family from America as a classic case of a family cursed.

One of the authors was teaching on this in Victoria (Australia) and finished by explaining about Dr. Prince's symptoms of a curse. As opportunity was given for prayer and ministry at the end of the meeting, two young ladies in their early twenties came forward, both crying. When asked what they required prayer for, they said that list was their family situation, all seven symptoms. A local pastor who knew how to handle these issues was invited to assist, along with the ladies' own pastor, as this would take a more than brief prayer at the meeting. Six weeks later we checked with the pastor, and he reported that the curses had been broken off their family, and forty-two members of that family had since come to salvation in Jesus Christ. Praise God!

Christians must be aware that curses are not the only causes of human problems. Problems may arise as a result of our own choice to sin. For example, sexual sins reap a harvest of viral and bacterial diseases, and abortions often result in emotional and spiritual problems.

One may ask, how can a curse operate in a Christian's life? The view is held by some that the sacrifice of Jesus did everything for us at Calvary. He said "It is finished!" That is very true. John wrote that those who **"... believe in Him shall not perish but have eternal life,"** (John 34:16). Also **"While we were still powerless Christ died for all,"** (Romans 5:6). These are true, but only half of the picture. Jesus Christ died for all, but not all receive eternal life and salvation. Jesus made the provision of salvation, but not everyone has or will repent of their sins and put their trust in Jesus Christ, and consequently they do not fulfil God's conditions for salvation. They will not be saved or inherit eternal life. Salvation is a free gift from God, but we have to receive it by fulfilling God's conditions, not of works but of repentance and surrender to Him.

Jesus covered the curses in the same way. **"Christ redeemed us from the curse of the Law, by becoming a curse for us..."** (Galatians 3:13). Jesus made the provision of release from curses, but again we have to appropriate what He did so we may be truly and fully free.

It is with the same reasoning that people have stated that a Christian cannot have demonic problems. But a Christian is not totally immune to demonic influence. Satan can trespass his way even into heaven (Job 1). That is how he became the accuser of the Brethren. (Revelation 12:10). We surely are under the Lord's protection, and no-one can just come along and hurt us or put a curse on us (John 10:27-28). But when we sin and refuse to repent, we open ourselves to attack, because in sin we are in disobedience to God. **"The curse without cause shall not alight,"** (Proverbs 26:2). 1 John 5:18 says if we keep ourselves from sin, the wicked one cannot touch us (i.e. cannot cling to us). If we are not in sin, the demonic presence is not legal, and God has provided for us a way of getting rid of the illegal spiritual squatter through repentance, renunciation, and deliverance.

Derek Prince likens a curse to a dam which holds back waters of blessing - all you get is just a trickle of blessings plus a lot of problems. God expects Christians to live according to Biblical principles. When we do that, no demon or curse may take hold of us. Judas Iscariot was an apostle, but he came under the title of "Son of Perdition," (John 17:12). Because he stole money from the disciples' purse suggests his life remained unchanged, and sin still ruled him. Ananias and Saphira were Christians but they allowed Satan to **"fill their hearts,"** (Acts 5:3). (Bible readers will know of these people and the consequences of their compromises.) There are many sinful actions that allow demons and curses to come into our lives. Here are the main ones.

Idolatry - Deuteronomy 27:15; Involvement in occultism or dabbling in witchcraft, divination, secret cults (e.g. Freemasonry, Mormonism, etc.), worship of idols, and unforgiveness (manifesting as hatred, anger or rebellion). This includes wrong and secret covenants and bringing occultic objects into our homes.

Dishonoring of Parents - Exodus 20:12; Dishonoring, disrespect, disobedience and rebellion against parents and caregivers.

Unconfessed personal sins - Deuteronomy 27:17-25; Sins of cheating, lying, financial dishonesty, backbiting (v 24).

Curses - put on people by those deeply involved in the occult, e.g. satanists, witchdoctors, e.g. Balaam (Numbers 22:4-6). An example of this has come to light. A former Vietnamese Buddhist monk has confessed that an entire sect of Buddhist monks spent much of the ***Vietnam War*** cursing all military servicemen in their country. The curses were very specific - that the soldiers etc. would be "wandering young men, angry and never finding peace." Psychiatrists and doctors gave it a name - ***"Post Traumatic Stress Syndrome."*** They admit they have no solution. One of the authors mentioned this Buddhist curse during a meeting in Australia. Following the meeting a man came forward, and after introducing himself he said he had been a Christian all his adult life, yet with tears in his eyes, he stated that I had just described the past 25 years of his life. Ministry was arranged for him immediately. Several other men who were also in Vietnam have also responded and been set free. Sadly, Islamic Mullahs (priests) from Iraq and Saudi Arabia did something similar during the Gulf War. Many Islamic Mullahs, during the five times for prayer daily, frequently curse all the "Infidels" (Christians and other non-Moslems). Apart from breaking the curses off, the Christian response must be to bless, and not to curse.

Curses due to false doctrines - Galatians 1:8-9; e.g. cults such as Mormons, Jehovah's Witnesses, Christadelphians, Spiritualism, etc., and false religions including Baha'i, Hinduism, Buddhism, Islam, etc.,

Involvement in Sexual Sins - Deuteronomy 27:20,23; incest, homosexuality & transvestism, (Romans 1:24-32) Adultery & fornication, (Romans 1:26,28,31).

Soul Ties - 2 Corinthians 6:14-17; Unequal yoking of people's souls such as is found among gangs, cult groups, secret societies such as Masonic and other lodges, New Age environmental and ecology groups which worship "Mother Earth" instead of Father God. Also Sexual soul-ties are established during fornication, adultery, bestiality and homosexuality, lesbianism and incest. Soul ties are spiritual knittings formed together between two souls that can either bring tremendous blessings in a Godly relationship (such as marriage) or tremendous destruction when made with the wrong person or group. In marriage there is the union of two people, but outside marriage is the devil's counterfeit of union and he establishes a link or channel between a man and woman in fornication etc. A type of cursed soul-tie may exist in a person and a previous spouse even after the marriage is dissolved, especially if the partner cheated on them.

Spoken curses - e.g. "You will never succeed in life," "You are useless."

Those who curse God's chosen - **"cursed be him who curses you,"** (Genesis 12:3). A real witch knows better than to attempt to curse a real Christian. Since **"a curse without cause shall not alight,"** (Proverbs 26:2); and **"No weapon formed against you (the Christian Believer) shall prosper,"** (Isaiah 54:17). Consequently a curse sent against a Christian who is truly walking with God will act like a boomerang, returning to afflict the originator and leaving the Christian untouched.

Inherited curses - often referred to as generational curses, sins of the fathers or ancestral curses. Certain sinful practices by that person often act as an opening for demonic invasion of a person. Such demons tend to travel down the blood lines, and given the right environments begin to afflict subsequent generations by means of curses or ancestral curses.

Exodus 20:4-5 says, **"You shall not make any graven image..."** God revealed Himself to Moses on Mt. Sinai as God who **"visits the sins of the fathers..."** (Exodus 34:7; & Numbers 14:18). This is not a habit pattern of sin or rebellion acquired from association with their parents, it is God's judgement visiting the children and grandchildren along the generational line. **"You who are left shall waste away in your iniquity in your enemies' lands, also in their fathers' iniquities, they shall waste away,"** (Leviticus 26:39).

Inherited curses may operate as repeated rejections, humiliations, barrenness and sicknesses in the family. Some inherited demons operate in people giving them a sense of having been there before, or "Deja vu." Ancestral curses/spirits because they have been in the family line for generations, can transfer some historic information to the current victim. Families with such curses tend to be attracted to the occult, witchcraft and spiritualism. Job 21:17-19 says, "God lays up one's iniquity for his children." Isaiah 14:21 says, "Prepare slaughter for his children because of the iniquity of their fathers..." Some inherited curses even go down to ten generations, (Deuteronomy 23:2). Due to sexual perversions by Ham (Genesis 9:18-27) his father Noah cursed his son Canaan to be a servant. Canaan's offspring became sexually perverted and his two major cities of Sodom and Gomorrah (Genesis 10;15-19) became so sexually immoral that God Himself had to bring down fire from heaven to destroy these cities.

Jeremiah 32:18 says, **"You show loving kindness to thousands, and repay the iniquity of the fathers into the bosom of their children after them..."** Some of these inherited "punishments" (curses/demons) manifest as psychic power, premonitions, occultic visions, mind-reading, psychic manifestations, down the generational line. Sometimes indicators of ancestral curses may include sex perversions, manifestations of familiar spirits, frigidity in marriage, unusual allergies, accident-prone life, spiritual blockages, religious delusions, compulsive thoughts, suicidal tendencies, repeated broken marriages down through a family's blood line. Other indications may include addictions, incest, mental and emotional breakdowns in the blood lines. **"Our fathers sinned and are no more, but we bear their iniquities,"** (Lamentations 5:7).

Ancestral curses or spirits are easily picked up at non-Christian funeral ceremonies, often involving "receiving the veil or the mantle." Family demons have been transferred through some types of inherited family objects such as the Masonic gowns and regalia passed on to a son, an old box used for occultic rituals or storing items or family treasures.

Ezekiel 18 gives balanced and detailed teaching about inherited curses. Israel had reached that place in their sins where they were blaming every current problem on the sins of their fathers. This is a dangerously extreme position to take. We are responsible for our own sins. We reap what we sow (Galatians 6:7). God spoke through the prophet Ezekiel to correct this blame-shifting. We need to reconcile that the wages of sin is death (Romans 6:23), with the fact that some sins we commit now may have long term repercussions on our children, grandchildren and our great grandchildren (Deuteronomy 5:9). Ezekiel gives the answer to sin, **"Repent and turn from all your transgressions, so that iniquity shall not be your ruin,"** (Ezekiel 18:30).

Experience by many Christian counselors shows that inherited curses can and do remain on a person, even after conversion. Many Christians have wondered why? The work of grace at Salvation does cleanse us and for some even heal us of many problems when we accept Christ as Lord and Savior. But the grace of God is made available to us during the time of salvation and for the rest of our Christian lives through specific gifted ministries (1 Corinthians 12; Romans 12; Mark 16:16-18) that help to rid us of any unresolved problems in our lives (including lingering curses). If curses are identified the person must be set free through appropriate ministry or deliverance prayer just the same way as when one is sick, the elders of the church lay hands on them, anoint them with oil and pray with them (James 5:14-15).

Galatians 3:13 says, **"Christ has redeemed us from the curse of the law, having become a curse for us..."** Christ's redemption covers our sins, sicknesses, and curses. It was completed 2,000 years ago on the cross of Calvary. Like forgiveness of sins we can only reap those benefits of the cross by personally accepting it by faith. Christ paid for our sicknesses with His stripes (wounds) (1 Peter 2:24) but we were healed when we trusted this finished work on the cross and prayed for healing. In the same manner we need to break curses in us as we trust Christ's finished work on the cross where He became a curse for us (Galatians 3:13). Colossians 2:14 says **"Having wiped out the handwriting of requirements that was against us, which was contrary to us. And He has taken it out of the way, having nailed it to the cross."**

(For much greater detail on this subject, one of the authors has since written ***"Dealing with Curses & Generational Iniquities,"*** listed at the end of this book.)

Hippocratic & Nursing Oaths

At the time of graduation, many medical schools and universities have an oath for the graduates. There are several versions of what has become known as "The Hippocratic Oath," and two versions are shown below. Because they reveal some interesting aspects we felt we should include both versions.

Version one

"I will look upon him who shall have taught me this Art even as one of my parents. I will share my substance with him, and I will supply his necessities, if he be in need. I will regard his offspring even as my own brethren, and I will teach them this Art, if they would learn it, without fee or covenant. I will impart this Art by precept, by lecture and by every mode of teaching, not only to my own sons, but to the sons of him who taught me, and to disciples bound by covenant and oath, according to the Law of Medicine.

"The regimen I adopt shall be for the benefit of my patients according to my ability and judgement, and not for their hurt or for any wrong. I will give no deadly drug to any, though it be asked of me, nor will I counsel such, and especially I will not aid a woman to procure abortion. Whatever house I enter, there will I go for the benefit of the sick, refraining from all wrongdoing or corruption, and especially from any act of seduction, of male or female, of bond or free. Whatsoever things I see or hear concerning the life of men, in my attendance on the sick, or even apart there from, which ought not to be noised abroad, I will keep silence thereon, counting such things to be as sacred secrets."[36]

Version Two

"I swear by Apollo the physician and Aesculapius and health and all the gods and goddesses that according to my ability and judgement I will keep this oath and its stipulation to reckon him who taught me this art equally dear to me as my parents; to share my substance with him and relieve his necessities if required; to look upon his offspring in the same footing as my own brothers and to teach them this art if they

a caduseus

wish to learn it without fees or stipulation; and that by precept, lecture and every other mode of instruction, I will impart a knowledge of the art to my own sons and those of my teachers and to disciples bound by a stipulation and oath according to the law of medicine but to none others.

"I will follow that system of regimen which, according to my ability and judgement I consider for the benefit of my patients, and abstain from whatever is deleterious and mischievous. I will give no deadly medicine to anyone if asked nor suggest such counsel, and in like manner I will not give to a woman a pessary to produce abortion. With purity and with holiness I will pass my life and practice my art.

"I will not cut persons labouring under the stones, but will leave this to be done by men who are practitioners of this work. Into whatever houses I enter, I will go into them for the benefit of the sick and will abstain from every voluntary act of mischief and corruption, and further, from the seduction of females or males, of freemen and slaves.

"Whatever, in connection with my professional practice, or not in connection with it, I see or hear, in the life of men, which ought not to be spoken abroad, I will not divulge as reckoning that all such should be kept secret.

"While I continue to keep this oath unviolated, may it be granted to me to enjoy life and the practice of the art, respected by all men, in all times, but should I trespass and violate this oath, may the reverse be my lot."

A number of medical people have confirmed there are other variations to this oath. Apart from the worthy and lofty ideals of integrity which both versions state so eloquently, there are a few points which need highlighting. These are oaths, whether they state this or not. They invoke judgement should the oath be broken. Of particular note is the absolute refusal to bring harm or death to a patient or to permit or encourage abortion. Secrets are also expected to be kept like a priest's confessional. A question put by someone who had read these was, "How many doctors have brought judgement curses on themselves through breaking these oaths, especially those who perform abortions?" There is a subsequent question which demands consideration; "Do those curses get transferred in some way onto other patients?" We believe this is possible.

What about these Greek gods mentioned in the second oath? Apollo is the god of medicine, destruction, archery, prophecy, music, and poetry, and represents the highest type of masculine beauty. The Greek word for 'destroy' is "apollumi," and Apollyon in the Bible means "The Destroyer" or "One who exterminates." According to Greek mythology, Apollo is the son of Zeus, (the king of gods) and his mother is Leto. His twin sister is the goddess Artemis, whom the Romans knew as Diana. The Romans also worshipped Apollo, and claimed he was the god of light, purity, the sun, and of sudden destruction. He was also a god of prophecy, and caused Pythia a prophetess to go into a trance and utter indistinct words. These words were interpreted by the priests in Apollo's temples. It was also claimed that he had the power to forgive sin, and this was before the time of Christ.

Aesculapius was Apollo's son. He was known as the god of healing, and his powers were said to be so great that he could bring the dead back to life. According to Greek mythology, this brought strife between Hades (the god of the dead) and Aesculapius who was seeking to cheat the kingdom of the dead of its inhabitants. Here we have two evil entities posing as mythical deities fighting over people to control them. Snakes were sacred to Aesculapius, and his insignia is known today as the caduceus. Sometimes this is known as the Staff of Mercury - a stick with two serpents entwining it. You will see the caduceus on most medical items to this day. Readers may wish to do their own research on these issues, but we wish to raise the matter of the rightness (or otherwise) of taking oaths to ancient and false deities. Any Christian who has been trained in medicine and who took any form of the Hippocratic Oath should consider which parts need to be prayerfully renounced before the Lord God, one of whose titles is Jehovah Rapha, "The God who heals." We can read elsewhere in Scripture that He is a jealous God who will not share His worship with any other.

Let us also turn briefly to a copy of an oath used by many New Zealand Registered Nurses, as shown by their insignia on the top. (See page 100.) They claim links to the Egyptian goddess Isis, and to the sun god,

The Five-Pointed Star, the recognised Badge of those connected with Medicine, originated with the Priests of the Temple of Isis, some thousands of years before Christ. The Priests of Isis became a powerful body of healing in the land, especially amongst the nomadic tribes of Egypt. To secure admission of reliable, worthy men, Oaths of Allegiance were sworn upon a representation of a Five-Pointed-Star, as emblematical of Ra (God) and a curative agency. Breaches of faith were punished by loss of limb, or even death.

The Hand

That my hand shall ever be extended to help, comfort and relieve the sick and suffering.

The Foot

That my feet shall not falter, loiter or linger, when journeying to alleviate the suffering of the sick.

The Knee

That my knee shall bow in supplication to the Almighty Creator Ra for guidance and aid in my endeavour to succour and relieve the sick and suffering.

The Breast

That my breast shall be a safe and sacred repository of any secret entrusted to me : or divulged during the sickness or delirium : or otherwise obtained.

The Head

That I will constantly pursue the study of the secret Arts. That I will exercise my knowledge to the benefit of those suffering mental or bodily distress, and that I will disseminate such knowledge among others that my preceptors may authorise and direct.

New Zealand Registered Nurses statement

"Almighty Creator Ra." This also is a counterfeit of the true God, and will need to be repented of by any Christian nurse who took the oath. Christian Evangelist Bill Subritzky (of Auckland, New Zealand) in his teaching on hindrances to healing, states that he had often wondered why when praying for nurses there was often no improvement in their health. Once he became aware of the oaths many nurses were require to take, there began to be some dramatic results when ministering with these people. Not all nurses have invoked such statements

Prayer And Action Of Renunciation

If you are or were ever involved in any aspect of the Alternative Health therapies discussed in this book, we recommend that you pray through the following prayer from your heart. Please read it through first so you know what is involved. It is best to pray this aloud with a Christian witness or counselor present. We suggest a brief pause following each paragraph to allow the Holy Spirit to show any additional issues which may require attention.

"Father God, creator of heaven and earth, I come to you in the name of Jesus Christ your Son. I come as a sinner seeking forgiveness and cleansing from all sins committed against you, and others made in your image. I honor my earthly father and mother and all of my ancestors of flesh and blood, and of the spirit by adoption and godparents, but I utterly turn away from and renounce all their sins and iniquities. I forgive all my ancestors for the effects of their sins on me and my children. I confess and renounce all of my own sins. I renounce and rebuke Satan and every spiritual power of his affecting me and my family.

I renounce and forsake all involvement in all forms of sorcery, divination, astrology, and any medical, holistic or alternative health therapy by my ancestors and myself. I renounce any and all treatments or therapies which have harmed my spirit or my soul, in the name of Jesus Christ.

In the name of Jesus Christ I now rebuke all evil curses, breaking their power, and I loose myself and my children from them; all inherited or ancestral curses, curses from others; all evil words spoken by parents, teachers, old friends, relatives, spouses, all witchcraft or voodoo assignments, and all curses stemming from my culture. I now break the power of all charms, hexes, spells, psychic powers, bewitchments, witchcraft, sorcery, incantations, impartations, or assignments that have been put upon me or my family line from any person or group, living or dead, or from any occult or psychic sources, including any familiar spirit assigned to me by Satan at my birth. I rebuke all connected and related spirits and command these to leave me now, in the mighty name of Jesus Christ.

I break every remaining soul tie that is ungodly with persons and groups in my past, in the name of Jesus Christ. I renounce the ungodly soul tie with (cult group - mention name); with (mention person's name) who led me into the occultism of Alternative Health Therapies, Astrology, Sorcery, Divination, (name practice); with the hypnotist (name); with (name) who led me into drugs; and with (name/s) that I had sinful sexual relations with (adultery, fornication, homosexuality, bestiality etc.) and also with the person whose blood was transfused into me.

I renounce all these and any other ungodly soul ties (mention other names that are appropriate) and I command the spirits attached to all these soul ties to leave me now in the name of Jesus Christ. I gather those ungodly soul ties together now and sever them through with the Sword of the Spirit of God, and I command them to never reattach. I now ask my Heavenly Father to reaffirm the appropriate Godly soul ties that I have with my spouse, children, and with members of the Body of Christ.

Now dear Father God, I ask humbly for the blood of Jesus Christ, your Son, to cleanse me from all these sins I have confessed and renounced, to cleanse my spirit, my soul, my mind, my emotions and every part of my body which has been affected by these sins, in Jesus' name!

I renounce every evil spirit associated with the Alternative Health areas and all other sins, and I command in the name of Jesus Christ for Satan and every evil spirit to be bound and to leave me now, touching or harming no-one, and go to the place appointed for you by the Lord Jesus, never to return to me or my family. I call on the name of the Lord Jesus to be delivered of these spirits, in accordance with the many promises of the Bible. I ask to be delivered of every spirit of sickness, infirmity, curse, affliction, addiction, disease or allergy associated with these sins I have confessed and renounced. I surrender to God's Holy Spirit and to no other spirit all the places in my life where these sins have been. I ask you, Lord, to baptise me in your Holy Spirit now according to the promises in your Word. I take to myself the whole armor of God in accordance with Ephesians Chapter Six, and rejoice in its protection as Jesus surrounds me and fills me with His Holy Spirit. I enthrone you, Lord Jesus, in my heart, for you are my Lord and my Saviour, the source of eternal life. Thank you, Father God, for your mercy, your forgiveness and your love, in the name of Jesus Christ, Amen."

If you have difficulty doing this, then please contact the authors, or a competent Christian leader near you, to assist you. Find Bible-believing Christians and spend time with them. Explain to them you are coming out of deception and need their encouragement and support at least until you are firmly on your feet. If some disappoint you (probably through not understanding your need) don't be put off, there are caring Christians around who can and will help. It is very important that you sever all of your ties with all Spiritualist and occult groups.

Occult Check List - Things To Repent Of

Amulets	Ankhs	Astral Travel
Astrology	Automatic Writing	Birth Signs
Black Magic	Chain Letters	Channeling
Charms	Clairaudience	Clairvoyance
Color Therapy	Crystal Balls	Crystal Power
Divining Rods	Divination	Dowsing
Dream Interpretation	Dungeons &Dragons	Eastern Meditation
E.S.P.	Fire Walking	Fortune Telling
Hallucinogenic Drugs	Handwriting Analysis	Heavy Metal Music
Hexagrams	Horoscopes	Hypnosis
Idols	Incantations	Iridology
Kabbala	Karma	Levitation
Lucky Charms	Magic	Mantras
Martial Arts	Mediums	Mesmerism
Metaphysics	Mind Control	Mind Reading
Necromancy	Numerology	Occult Literature
Omens	Ouija Boards	Pagan Objects
Palm Reading	Parapsychology	Pendulums
Psychic Healing	Psychometry	Punk Rock Music
Pyramid Power	Rebirthing	Reincarnation
Satanism	Seances	Self Hypnosis
Silva Mind Control	Sorcery	Soul Travel
Spells	Star Signs	Superstitions
Talismans	Tarot Cards	Tea Leaf Reading
Telepathy	T. M.	Trances
UFO's	White Magic	Yoga
Zodiac Signs		

How To Help Those In The Occult

Christians should not be fearful of those involved in the occult. These people are lost and need to be shown how to find Jesus Christ. Show them the scripture in Deuteronomy 18 where God condemns witchcraft, then show them Galatians 5:19 - 20 which confirms that. Then show them there is now no condemnation in Christ Jesus if they repent of their sin and accept Jesus as Lord of all. God says they will become a new creation in Christ by doing this. Don't argue theology because they usually know about that. What they really need is to meet the real Jesus. A former Wiccan leader who now runs a Christian ministry to reach those in witchcraft and related groups says that any Christian who is afraid to witness to a witch needs to go back to their Bible and learn it properly.

How To Pray Effectively For Occultists

* The first matter to understand is that the battle is spiritual. **"For we do not wrestle against flesh and blood (your relative/friend) but against principalities, against powers, against the rulers of darkness of this age, against spiritual hosts of wickedness in heavenly places"** (Ephesians 6:12). You are not fighting your loved one. They are in spiritual bondage. You are going to deal with the demonic spirits which blind and deafen them to the true Gospel of Jesus Christ, and which prevent them responding to Him.

* Make sure there is no unconfessed sin in your life. If there is, get right with God. Then know your authority in Christ to overcome all the power of the evil one. **"I give you the authority to trample on serpents and scorpions (demons), and over all the power of the enemy, and nothing shall by any means hurt you. Nevertheless, do not rejoice in this, that the spirits are subject to you, but rather rejoice because your names are written in heaven"** (Luke 10:19-20).

* If possible, ask another Christian believer to agree with you in prayer. **"...If two of you agree on earth concerning anything you**

ask, it will be done for you by My Father in heaven" (Matthew 18:19). What if you are alone, and have no-one to agree with you? Lorri MacGregor (a former cult member who now heads up a Christian ministry to reach people in cults) recommends you ask Jesus or the Holy Spirit to agree with you. Then pray to God in the name of the Savior Jesus Christ as the Holy Spirit directs you.

* Bind all the demonic strongmen, in the name of Jesus Christ. **"Assuredly, I say to you, whatever you bind on earth will be bound in heaven..."** (Matthew 18:18). Ask the Holy Spirit for the names of, or effects caused by, these and other demonic spirits, and how to remove their influence from your friend or relative. Ask God to release and loose them from these demonic spirits and all others which control them. **"...Whatever you loose on earth will be loosed in heaven"** (Matthew 18:18). Also you will need to break, in the name of Jesus Christ, every curse, (including all ancestral or inherited curses) which the person is under.

* Be assured that God is now at work in their lives to release them from their bondage. Pray for their salvation, in faith. If the person is a family member, God's promise to you is to **"Believe on the Lord Jesus Christ, and you shall be saved, you and your household"** (Acts 16:31). If they are not a family member, God gives another promise for you to appropriate in prayer for them. **"The Lord is not slack concerning His promise ...but is longsuffering towards us, not willing that any should perish but that all should come to repentance"** (2 Peter 3:9) and **"God our Savior... desires all men to be saved and to come to the knowledge of the truth"** (1 Timothy, 2:4). God's Word is plain, He doesn't want your relative or friend to perish. God wants them saved, and we have a commission from Him to find out how, and then to do the job in prayer.

* Keep on praying in faith for your relative or friend. Experience shows that perseverance produces the best results, so don't be discouraged if there are no positive signs for a while. Ask the Lord to make Himself known to them and to make His word alive to them.

References

1 "Healing at any Price", by Dr. Samuel Pfeifer, p 89-90

2 Quoted by "Can You Trust Your Doctor," by John Ankerberg & Dr. John Weldon, pps 53-54

3 For example, "Can you Trust Your Doctor?" Ankerberg and Weldon 1991 pps 1-11

4 "Alternative Health Care," by Professor Patrick Pietroni, (CLB Publishing) 1995 P 9,

5 Monism is the denial of matter. Pantheism is the belief that everything which exists is God.

6 "Psychic Forces & Occult Shock," by Clifford Wilson & Dr. John Weldon p 268

7 "Acupuncture Diagnosed - Points of Contention," by Tony Bambridge, P 62

8 "Homeopathy Diagnosed - Powerful Water," by Tony Bambridge, Pps 70-73

9 "Finding a Natural Alternative," NZ Women's Weekly, December 19, 1988.

10 "Hypnotism Investigated," by Tony Bambridge, P. 132

11 "Hypnotism Investigated," by Tony Bambridge, p 130-135

12 "Acupuncture Diagnosed - Points of Contention," by Tony Bambridge, p 57.

13 "Homeopathy Diagnosed - Powerful Water," by Tony Bambridge, Pps 66-70

14 "Directions" - a directory of holistic health, 1996 edition p 14

15 "Cultwatch," by Dr. John Ankerberg & Dr. John Weldon, p 172

15a "Encyclopedia of New Age Beliefs," by Dr. John Ankerberg & Dr. John Weldon, p 80

16 "The Facts on Holistic Health," by John Ankerberg & Dr. John Weldon, P. 20

17 "Occult ABC," by Dr. Kurt Koch, pps 42,43

18 source - Fr. Mitch Pacwa, S.J.; Catholic Circle Magazine, August 16, 1992)

19 "Homoeopathy - some things are not what they seem," by Branson Hopkins, p 13

20 "Understanding More Alternative Medicine," by Roy Livesey, p 75

21 "Psychic Forces & Occult Shock," by Clifford Wilson & Dr. John Weldon pps 227-228

22 "Occult ABC," by Dr. Kurt Koch, pps 95-100

23 "Healing at any Price," by Samuel Pfeifer, p 89-90

24 "The Facts on Holistic Health," by John Ankerberg & Dr. John Weldon, p 33

25 "Alternative Health Care," by Professor Patrick Pietroni, (CLB Publishing) 1995 p 50

26 "Directions" - a directory of holistic health, 1996 edition p 56

27 "Hypnotism Investigated," by Tony Bambridge, P. 139

28 "Occult ABC," by Dr. Kurt Koch, pps 152-154

29 "Directions" - a directory of holistic health, 1996 edition. p 80

30 "Psychic Forces & Occult Shock," by Clifford Wilson & Dr. John Weldon. p.

31 "Understanding More Alternative Medicine," by Roy Livesey, p 190

32 "Can You Trust Your Doctor," by John Ankerberg & Dr. John Weldon pps 33-35

33 "Hindrances to Healing" - Bill Subritzky video/audio teaching

34 "Healing" by Francis MacNutt pps 248-261

35 "Blessing or Curse - you can choose," by Dr. Derek Prince, p. 45

36 "Family Health Guide", Reader's Digest, Sydney, 3rd edition, 1979

37 "The Facts on Holistic Health" by Dr. John Ankerberg & Dr. John Weldon, p 20

38 "Healing For Your Hurts" by Dr. Hendrik Visser M.D.

Recommended Reading

We have gleaned much of our material from many books, audio and video tapes as well as conversations and interviews with many people. Some sources we cannot recommend but the following list provide some of the best information which we are pleased to commend to the reader if they are seeking the truth.

"Can You Trust Your Doctor," by John Ankerberg & Dr. John Weldon, (Wolgemuth & Hyatt)

"Encyclopedia of New Age Beliefs," by John Ankerberg & Dr. John Weldon, (Harvest House)

"Psychic Forces & Occult Shock," by Clifford Wilson & Dr. John Weldon, (Global Publishers)

"Healing For Your Hurts" by Dr. Hendrik Visser MD

"Healing at any Price," by Samuel Pfeifer, M.D., (Word Books)

"Understanding More Alternative Medicine," by Roy Livesey, (New Wine Press)

"Biblical Healing Training Manual" by Dr. Selwyn Stevens, (Jubilee)

"The Reiki Danger - Healing that Harms" by E S Harz, (Jubilee)

"Acupuncture Diagnosed - Points of Contention," by Tony Bambridge, (Jubilee)

"Hypnotism Investigated," by Tony Bambridge, (New Wine Press)

"Homeopathy Diagnosed - Powerful Water," by Tony Bambridge, (Jubilee)

"Homoeopathy - some things are not what they seem," by Branson Hopkins, (Jubilee)

"Insights into Martial Arts, Tai Ch'i, TM & Yoga," by Dr. Selwyn Stevens, (Jubilee)

"What the Bible says about Healthy Living," by Rex Russell, M.D., (Regal Books)

"Testing the Spirits," by Elizabeth L. Hillstrom, (InterVarsity Press)

"The New Age is Lying to You," by Eldon K. Winker, (Concordia Publishing House)

"Occult ABC," by Dr. Kurt Koch, (Literature Mission Aglasterhausen)

"The Facts on Holistic Health," by John Ankerberg & Dr. John Weldon, (Harvest House)

"Cultwatch - what you need to know about spiritual deception," by John Ankerberg & Dr. John Weldon, (Harvest House)

"Healing" & "The Power To Heal," by Francis MacNutt (Ave Maria Press)

"Where is God when It Hurts," by Philip Yancey, (Zondervan)

"When God Doesn't Make Sense," by Dr. James Dobson, (Tyndale House)

"Blessing or Curse," by Dr. Derek Prince, (Chosen Books)

"Evicting Demonic Squatters & Breaking Bondages," by Noel & Phyl. Gibson, (Freedom in Christ)

"None of These Diseases," by S.I. McMillen, (Fleming H. Revell)

"How You Can be Healed," by Gordon Lindsay, (Christ for the Nations)

"Handbook for Healing," by Charles & Frances Hunter (Hunter Books)

"Healing in Every Book of the Bible," by Lester Sumrall, (Lesea Publications)

"Scripture Keys for Kingdom Living," by June N. Davis, (Scripture Keys Ministries)

"I Believe in Miracles," by Kathryn Kuhlman, (Fleming H. Revell)

"How You Can Heal the Sick," by Stuart Gramenz, (Sovereign World)

"A More Excellent Way" by Dr. Henry W. Wright (Pleasant Valley Publications)

Summary - We Each Have a Choice!

It all comes back to one decision - do you choose to believe the Bible or not? Those whose choice is to reject the Bible and all it contains, despite the overwhelming evidence of its reliability, have consequences to face some time in the future, maybe sooner than they think.

What if

* the Bible is not true?

* there isn't a creator God?

* Jesus isn't the only savior?

* there is no such thing as sin, therefore no judgement for sin either?

What would someone lose if they believed the Bible, yet it was later proved wrong? Personally I doubt they would lose much, because the morality of parts such as the Ten Commandments and Jesus' teaching about loving others would, if lived out, make this world a better place. That person would also have a sense of personal worth and integrity.

But if

* the Bible is true;

* a creator God did make each of us in His own image;

* Jesus really did die for our sins and to restore our relationship with God,

* Jesus is coming again soon;

* there is a Judgement Day where we must each give an account;

* the result of that Judgement Day is an eternal existence either in heaven with God or in hell without Him,

Then what do we stand to lose if all this is true yet we reject it?

Effectively we each have three votes. God has one which He has cast for our eternal benefit. Satan has one which he has cast for our eternal destruction. Every human being has the last vote, and must choose to vote with God or Satan - so we get the casting vote. Who will you vote for?

You, the reader, now have a choice to make

About Jubilee Resources International

God's commission for Jubilee Resources International is based on Ezekiel 33:1-9, and Luke 4:18-21. According to the Bible, Jubilee years were times of restitution. Debts were cancelled, slaves set free, families reunited and lost or forfeited inheritances restored. Every year was prophetic of the ministry of Jesus Christ. The Jubilee was proclaimed on the basis of the work of the High Priest on the Day of Atonement - so Jesus Christ's liberating ministry is founded on His atoning work. Jesus began His public ministry by reading the passage from the prophet Isaiah (Luke 4:18-21). All the liberties of the Jubilee year are now available to us through the redemptive work of Jesus Christ at Calvary, and we all have the responsibility to preach this Gospel of Redemption and Restoration to full Relationship with Yahweh/Father God. When Yeshua/Jesus Christ returns, God's people will be totally free from all sin, sickness and disease, death and curse. The Biblical Jubilee will then be fully realized.

Resources in print book, eBook, audio & video formats are available in English, with paper & eBooks in Spanish, German, French, Italian, Portuguese-Brazil, Polish, Russian, Dutch, Swedish, Danish, Finnish, Hungarian, Romanian, Slovak, Czech, Greek, Afrikaans & Tagalog, with other languages pending.

Additional Resources Available by

Selwyn R. Stevens

www.jubileeresources.org (Webshop)

Plus comprehensive range of free tracts to download

Dealing with Curses & Generational Iniquities. This teaching offers hope for all Christians that they can be released into the blessings of God and forever leave behind iniquities and curses that have kept them captive, perhaps their whole families for generations. This explains the twelve major curses that people may have operating in their families, and what to do about them. It also includes new material on the curses over Scottish, English, Irish, Welsh and Scandinavian people, plus many other national and ethnic groups. This teaching has been taught in several nations with much fruit for personal, family and community liberty. Best Seller
Book, E-book, MP4 & DVD

Dealing with Demons: *Insights into evil spiritual influences.* This popular teaching provides outstanding insights regarding evil spiritual influences that exist in the world in which we live today, and then goes further to show us what to do about it. Best Seller
Book, E-book, MP4 & DVD

Insights into Martial Arts, Tai Ch'i TM & Yoga. Much of the western world has seen an explosion of these practices. For many, their involvement has became close to a religion, adopting belief systems, mind sets and practises inconsistent with the teachings of the Bible. Best Seller
Book, E-book, MP4 & DVD

Treated or Tricked - Alternative Health Therapies Diagnosed. Many people are now trying Alternative Health Therapies. This book explains the various medical & spiritual healing methods; investigates whether the "Energy/Life Force" is scientific or spiritual; and describes almost 80 different Alternative Therapies, from Aromatherapy to Zone therapies. Also examines reasons why some are not healed & how to overcome these failures Biblically. Co-authored with Dr. Badu Bediako, (former Assoc. Professor of BioChemistry.) Best Seller
Book, E-book, MP4 & DVD

How to Recognize the Voice of God. How does God communicate to His people? How will you know when it is Him speaking to you? This very practical teaching has already helped many.
Book & DVD

Raising a Blessed Generation. The goals of this teaching are three-fold:

Goal 1: To understand what Blessing is and the Power it has for our lives today;

Goal 2: To Identify and Recover any missed blessings in my own life;
Goal 3: To Begin to Learn How to Bless others, especially our children & grandchildren! Identity and gender confusion is caused by the failure of parents & grandparents to speak identity and destiny into the young ones. Best Seller
Book, E-book, MP4 & DVD

Daniel and the Star Chasers. The counterfeit of Astrology has hidden what God wanted His people to know about the Gospel message in the stars. Daniel taught that truth to the Magi of Asia, and that nearly caused the War of the Continents half a millennium later. Only in recent decades has mankind had the technology to uncover what the Magi saw. Following Daniel's instructions, they went to see the King of Kings and submit their kingdoms and empires to His.
Book, E-book, MP4 & DVD

The Christian Life & the Role of the Fivefold Ministry. The Christian church is being increasingly side-lined in social debate. Have we ceased to be the Salt and Light commanded by Jesus Christ? The Solution: become real Christians! But what does that entail? Then, how are Christians to be governed? God provided the Fivefold ministry to do that. What does that look like? Best Seller
Book, E-book, MP4 & DVD

Help! The Sheep are Escaping: Understanding the Exodus From Church to God's Ecclesia. For most Christians in the West, "church" isn't working! The Old Wineskin cannot compete any longer, as God raises up His New Wineskin to fulfil His end-time purposes. The solution is for "church" to become Ecclesia and for participation with appropriate equipping, releasing and accountability.
Book, E-book, MP4 & DVD

Biblical Healing Training Manual. This thorough examination of Biblical physical healing is the result of many years of experience as well as training under some of the world's best Bible teachers. There are many "How To's", practical prayer and ministry guidelines, reasons why some aren't healed, and what we can do about them, etc. Hundreds have been healed, & many congregations have been empowered to commence regular Healing services with Christ-glorifying results. Best Seller
Book, E-book, MP4 & DVD

Fatal Faith - the Cult Counterfeit of Christianity. This book explains how cults develop and what patterns to avoid. Key Christian and Cult beliefs are compared with the main active cults. How to handle door-knockers, cult exiting, pre-cult spiritually-abusive churches; and how to protect young people from cults. Major ancient & modern heresies examined. Best Seller.
Book, E-book

The New Age - the Old Lie in a New Package. New Age & Bible beliefs and practices compared, including Reincarnation and Past lives, Astrology, the New Age pseudo Messiah, Self-worship & our Deity-potential. Energy/ Life Forces are examined, and the occult involvement of most holistic health gurus. Best Seller
Book, E-book

Discerning the Past to See the End Times: *Islam's Role in the Return of Jesus*. The statue in Nebuchadnezzar's dream, interpreted by Daniel, gives us a clear picture of the various empires that have sought domination of the Middle East and beyond. World events circle around this area of vital interest to God and His people. The Bible is a Middle Eastern book, not a European or American book. The context of the empires of the statue give us vital clues about the Empire of the Beast to come! Best Seller
Book, E-book, MP4 & DVD

Signs & Symbols: Cult, New Age & Occult Insignias & What They Mean. From Ananda Marga, Anarchy, & Ankhs, to Yin & Yang, Yoga & Zodiacs. By popular demand this book has a brief explanation & a Biblical comparison with dozens of insignias. 7th Edition, newly revised. Best Seller
Book, E-book

How to Minister to Change Lives and Communities. This comprehensive & practical training manual is for those who want to do effective ministry. This can include end-of-service and small-group ministry. Topics include Understanding the Spiritual Realm; Empowerment to Serve; Healing of the Body, & the Soul; Deeper Ministry by appointment & referral; & Biblical blessings to release identity and destiny. Best Seller
Book, E-book, MP4 & DVD

The Bible 101. A teaching manual introducing the Bible, explaining clearly it's purposes, origins, history, inspiration, symbolism, translations & versions, moving from milk to meat, study helps, rules of interpretation, and how to study it to get the best understanding.
Book, E-book, & MP4

Unmasking Freemasonry - Removing the Hoodwink. Written primarily for the wives & families of Masons to explain the curses brought on themselves and their families through the oaths; then learn how to deal with the effects. History & structure are explained simply. A Past Master who read this book immediately resigned from his Lodge. The prayer guidelines from this book are being used by many ministries worldwide. 7th edition with endorsement by C. Peter Wagner. Best Seller
Book, E-book, MP4 & DVD

Unmasking Mormonism - Who are the Latter-day Saints? Learn about LDS founder Joseph Smith on whose credentials this cult fails Bible tests, the Book of Mormon hoax, Mormon polytheism, true & false priesthood & authority. This book has caused many Mormons to cancel their baptisms & leave to seek the genuine Jesus Christ - the One from the Bible. Best Seller
Book, E-book, MP4 & DVD

Unmasking the Watchtower - Who are the Jehovah's Witnesses? This asks the questions many J.W.'s are being expelled for daring to ask! Check out the changeable prophecies and man-made doctrines of the Watchtower, the authoritarian leaders & their use of Mind-Control & manipulation of members, how to know the One True God, and how you can witness to and pray for a J.W. effectively. Best Seller
Book, E-book, MP4 & DVD

Rome's Anathemas: Insights into the Papal Pantheon. This vital book investigates Constantine's divorce of the Jewish roots of the Christian faith and its replacement with paganism; the Council of Trent rejected the Biblical basis of Luther's Reformation and cursed all who disagreed with them. In John, we read of the marriage feast at Cana. Realizing that the wine was gone and that she herself could not do anything, Mary tells Jesus, because He is the only One who could do something. Mary then gives the stewards her last recorded words and only command - one that we must consider for us to be saved. Mary said, *"Whatever He say to you, do it!"*
Book, E-book, MP4 & DVD

Additional Resources Available by

Selwyn R. Stevens

www.jubileeresources.org (Webshop)

Plus comprehensive range of free tracts to download

Made in the USA
Columbia, SC
14 September 2024

42326126R00076